Daily Strength for Couples

A 365-DAY DEVOTIONAL

BroadStreet
PUBLISHING

BroadStreet Publishing Group, LLC.
Savage, Minnesota USA
Broadstreetpublishing.com

Daily Strength for Couples

© 2021 by BroadStreet Publishing

978-1-4245-6238-1 (faux)
978-1-4245-6239-8 (eBook)

Devotional entries compiled by Michelle Winger.

Design by Chris Garborg | garborgdesign.com
Compiled and edited by Michelle Winger | literallyprecise.com

Printed in China.

21 22 23 24 25 26   7 6 5 4 3 2 1

"Love each other deeply,

as much as I have loved you."

JOHN 15:12 TPT

Introduction

With your lives moving in fast forward and no known chance of slowing down, finding time to devote to your marriage can seem nearly impossible. Quality time is incredibly important for maintaining a healthy marriage in this quick-paced society where you run (sometimes literally) from errands to appointments to activities and back again.

One of the best ways to strengthen your relationship is to spend time with God—together.

This daily devotional offers inspiring reflections on relationships, encouraging Scriptures, and thought-provoking questions to help you intentionally engage with God and each other. When you prioritize spending a few moments to grow together in your relationship with God, you will quickly learn that it is the best way to begin or end your day.

January

A man shall leave his father and mother
and hold fast to his wife,
and they shall become one flesh.

GENESIS 2:24 ESV

Resolutions

I will give heed to the blameless way.
When will you come to me?
I will walk within my house in the integrity of my heart.
I will set no worthless thing before my eyes;
I hate the work of those who fall away;
It shall not fasten its grip on me.

PSALM 101:2-3 NASB

*M*any of us make annual New Year's resolutions, only to abandon them while the year is still young. The resolutions are usually great goals, but we lack the willpower to keep them. In Psalm 101, King David speaks boldly about his resolve to govern his kingdom and his home with integrity and righteousness.

Have you considered making the same declarations for your home and your marriage? Would your behavior, attitudes, words, and choice of movies and entertainment change? Would you be more mindful of keeping your word and be less influenced by the world? We know that determination alone cannot carry us, but David knew that too. He could make these bold statements because he knew that God was loving, kind, fair, and dependable. God is the real power behind resolutions.

Are the two of you willing to make David's resolutions your own?
How can you walk with integrity in every area of your life?

Life Adventures

How blessed is the man whose strength is in You,
In whose heart are the highways to Zion!
PSALM 84:5 NASB

*M*arriage is an adventure. Adventures take us into unknown territories, and so do our relationships. Part of the fun in any adventure is having a companion along for the journey, and nothing could be better than experiencing joyful moments with a sweetheart.

However, adventures come with hazards and unexpected moments that threaten to wreck our trips. Life adventures deal with unexpected heartache, health problems, and financial difficulties. Where do we turn when life's trip takes a bad turn? Tour guides lead and advise travelers on their adventures, and we have the ultimate guide in God. When troubles disrupt the adventure, he sees clearly our path, and he will provide the necessary tools for the journey.

What are some adventures that we can do together for God?
What have we learned from life adventure disruptions, and
how can we use those moments to draw closer to each other?

Thinking of You

God is my witness, how I long for you all
with the affection of Christ Jesus.
PHILIPPIANS 1:8 NASB

Built into each of us is a craving for love and affection, and that longing is important in our relationships. God set the standard for perfect love, inspiring us with his example. But it's easy to get busy or preoccupied as responsibilities claim our attention. Forgetting to express affection creates a void in our marriages.

Marriage needs all kinds of affection. Physical touch is vital; hugs and kisses say, "You are the most special person on earth to me." And it's important to hear the words *I love you* each day. Try writing a quick note to leave by your spouse's morning coffee cup. Send flowers just because, or a text that says, "Thinking of you." As God beautifully shares his love with us, we can become extensions of his loving hands and heart and share that love with the partner he's given us.

How do you feel when your sweetheart is affectionate toward you? What can you do to be more loving to your spouse?

Eternal Authority

> Even from eternity I am He,
> And there is none who can deliver out of My hand;
> I act and who can reverse it?
>
> ISAIAH 43:13 NASB

How glorious it is to belong to the King! What an honor to be counted among his children, to be held secure in his hand, to be the recipients of his love and affection. We are finite beings, but the Lord Almighty is infinite. Our presence here is fixed, but he is eternal. We were created by him and for him; he is the Author and Creator of all that we know. What he has decided to do, none can dismantle. Whom he decides to save, none can sway.

The Lord extends his hand and delivers us from our adversary, and all the enemy's schemes cannot crush his limitless power. He is from eternity, possessing all form of love and wisdom. His plan is perfect, and we are part of it. For all of time—past, present, and future—the Lord reigns with justice and mercy. We are blessed beyond measure to know and be known by him.

Knowing that God holds you and keeps you safe,
what could you and your spouse endeavor to do with boldness?

Foresight

I know that You can do all things,
And that no purpose of Yours can be thwarted.
JOB 42:2 NASB

Sitting in agony, covered in dust, boils, and tears, Job declared his faith in God. Although it seemed like his whole world had fallen apart, Job still believed that God was able to do anything. He believed in God's ability to remove his sufferings, yet he received something far greater than relief: God met Job in his pain and showed him his great mysteries. Rather than ease his suffering, he used it to open Job's eyes and grew his relationship with him even deeper! Job's faith multiplied, as did his wisdom.

When we suffer, rather than immediately seeking an escape, we should look for how the Lord might be using the situation to richly bless our lives. Instead of making our anguish end, he may meet us in it and share the burden with us. Far more desirable than a life of ease is the experience of a true friendship with the Creator. His plans will be established across the globe because his purposes cannot be stopped. His friends are invited to participate in his mission, but it will be accompanied by many hardships and trials. But he is with us through it all.

*In the midst of suffering, does your mind go first
to easing your pain or seeking God?
How can you encourage your spouse in moments of suffering?*

Best Friends

A friend is always loyal,
and a brother is born to help in time of need.

PROVERBS 17:17 NLT

True friendships are often revealed through adversity. When the excitement wears off and the trials hit, loyal friends will remain to help fight the battles. Their love is constant and not dependent on what they receive from the relationship. Friendship does not ask what is fair; it exhibits true love regardless of the cost.

Marriages will experience conflict, but a healthy marriage will rise above the argument and spouses will support each other through the best and worst of life. Christ is the perfect example of a devout lover, a brother, and a true friend. His love is constant, never wavering and eternal. He came to earth to help those in need, not to be served, and he gave his own life to serve those he loved. In Christ, we are family. We may be friends as well, but first we are brothers and sisters in Christ, loyal to the Lord and to each other.

Beyond partnership, do you and your spouse
enjoy a friendship together?

What You Bring

> You are a chosen race, a royal priesthood, a holy nation, God's own people,
> in order that you may proclaim the mighty acts of him who called you out
> of darkness into his marvelous light.
>
> 1 PETER 2:9 NRSV

We were chosen as God's people, and the purpose for that is not our own self-preservation or glorification, but so we may proclaim his goodness and explain all the incredible wonders he has done on our behalf. Remembering where we came from helps us keep perspective on who we are; we were once lost in darkness, but God called us out of it and flooded us with his marvelous light. Now we are members of his holy family.

Anyone willing to leave their dark pasts behind and submit themselves to Christ's calling becomes a member of his holy nation—a nation which will endure forever and not be swept away with temporal things. Regardless of where we come from or what we look like, we become one spiritual race since we share the same Father. Peter made it clear that this was not an invitation to the Israelites alone but to anyone who stumbled out of darkness and embraced living in God's light.

What opportunities do you have to proclaim
the mighty acts of God?

Stormy Waters

We also glory in our sufferings, because we know that suffering produces
perseverance; perseverance, character; and character, hope. And hope
does not put us to shame, because God's love has been poured out into our
hearts through the Holy Spirit, who has been given to us.

ROMANS 5:3-5 NIV

Wouldn't it be nice if every marriage came equipped with a
plan for smooth sailing? Instead, we encounter severe storms and
rough waters as we face financial difficulties, health crisis situations,
and relationship struggles. These moments can strengthen us or
destroy us, and our attitudes influence the outcome as we face those
challenges.

By asking God what he wants us to learn from those situations, we
build perseverance and character to help us in future storms. As we
see God's hand in our lives and marriages, we have confidence in
his will for the years ahead. And when we ride out those challenges
together as a couple, our love grows.

How do you react to challenges?
How can you work together
as a couple when stormy times arrive?

Precious

Let it be the hidden person of the heart,
with the imperishable quality of a gentle and quiet spirit,
which is precious in the sight of God.

1 PETER 3:4 NASB

*T*urning his attention specifically to Christian wives, Peter explained that a woman's true beauty is found in her unseen character rather than her outward appearance. Women are inundated with messages about what the world deems attractive, and they are plagued with insurmountable physical standards. Instead of striving to achieve some form of impossible physique, their focus should be on cultivating a humble and quiet heart. Like so many of the Bible's lessons which were directed at a certain group of people in that time, there are spiritual insights associated with them that are applicable to anyone.

To possess a "quiet spirit" does not mean women should stay silent, but that they ought to strive to maintain a level of inner peace and contentment which is only possible through relying on the Lord. In a world which applauds impenetrable toughness and caters to the loudest voices, Christians are to follow Christ's example by remaining caring and calm. Hardening your heart does not demonstrate a tenderness before the Lord, nor does anxiety and strife reveal a person who rests in God's peace. It is your hidden godly qualities that are precious to God.

How can you be calm when others around you are not?
How can you encourage your spouse to have a quiet spirit?

Understanding

As the heavens are higher than the earth,
so are my ways higher than your ways,
and my thoughts than your thoughts.

ISAIAH 55:9 NKJV

Have you and your spouse ever enjoyed God's handiwork in the sky? Blue skies and puffy white clouds are gorgeous. And there's something almost magical about a full moon and thousands of bright stars spread across the dark canopy of the sky. Those are the moments that make us understand what a big God we have.

Times like those are reminders that we shouldn't limit God when it comes to the dreams on our hearts. His dreams for us are always bigger than ours. If we'll listen to and understand his sweet whispers to us and follow through on those, we can achieve things as a couple that will be beyond our wildest expectations. He's equipped us with unique skills and life experiences, and it's such a joy to see the Lord use our spouse's life in a big way for God's glory.

Have you ever thought about what a big God we have?
How do we limit him by looking at our resources instead of his?

Hope Overflowing

May the God of hope fill you with all joy and peace as you trust in him,
so that you may overflow with hope by the power of the Holy Spirit.

ROMANS 15:13 NIV

Daily life is difficult, and we are easily ensnared by evils which attempt to tear us apart and distract us from what Yahweh has called us to do. He alone can offer us true hope, peace, and joy, so we must continue to trust him and block out contradictory voices. If we truly want to be upheld by his mighty hand, to be led by his Holy Spirit, and to be filled with his confident hope, then we need to put our trust solely in him.

We will see God work through our lives for the purpose of his pleasure if we are willing to use our God-given gifts to encourage and strengthen each other. In our relationships with our spouses, we ought to strive to put them before ourselves and to always put the Lord first. He is faithful to guide us and keep us, to give us strength when we have none, and to provide us with hope and peace. His Holy Spirit fills us so we can live to the full extent of the purposes he has set in place for us.

How does trust lead to joy and peace?

Living Sacrifice

I plead with you to give your bodies to God because of all he has done for you. Let them be a living and holy sacrifice—the kind he will find acceptable. This is truly the way to worship him.

ROMANS 12:1 NLT

The mercies of God surround us! Every moment of our lives is a gift we do not deserve. When we were worthy of death, he gave us forgiveness and life. He no longer demands animal sacrifices as an atonement for our sins but asks that we be fully committed to him in mind and body. Rather than the blood of goats, which served as a tangible example of the gravity and penalty of sin, he wants our full submission to him: our entire bodies, hearts, minds, and strength.

The Lord desires that we live for him in all that we say, think, and do. It is an unfathomable, undeserved gift that we no longer need to atone for our sins with sacrifices and offerings since he already settled that account for us by offering himself as the ultimate sacrifice. Since he bought and paid for us, we are fully his. Even more incredible is the fact that we are what he desires! He does not want sacrifices or servanthood but mutual love and devotion. May our lives be an act of worship to him because of all he has done for us.

What does it mean to be a living and holy sacrifice to the Lord in your daily life? How about in your marriage?

Good Gifts

*Who forbid marriage and require abstinence from foods that God created
to be received with thanksgiving by those who believe and know the truth.
For everything created by God is good, and nothing is to be rejected if it is
received with thanksgiving, for it is made holy by the word of God and prayer.*

1 TIMOTHY 4:3-5 ESV

Gnosticism teaches that all forms of physical pleasure are
inherently evil, including music and entertainment, delicious foods,
and sexual enjoyment. This sort of belief was trending at the time Paul
wrote to Timothy especially in Ephesus. He warned him against such
notions and reminded him that everything God created was good.

We are not supposed to reject the gifts of God but thank him for
them and enjoy them. He created so many things for our enjoyment
because he is a good and loving God. The popular practice of
Asceticism was also on the rise, which taught that by rejecting
pleasures of the flesh, people could avoid corruption and somehow
obtain a higher level of spirituality. Although nothing should
come before God in our lives, true holy living can only be attained
through spending time with God and in his Word because holiness
comes from him alone. Pride and self-reliance will corrupt us far
faster than enjoying God's blessings. Marriage is a gift from our
Maker to be treasured and enjoyed.

What sort of pleasures has God given you to enjoy?

The Great Need

*I am a friend to anyone who fears you—
anyone who obeys your commandments.*

PSALM 119:63 NLT

*M*utual interest is bonding. We share a connection with those who strive for the same things we do. The fear of the Lord leads us to wisdom, and a wise person will surround themselves with other wise people. Those who fear the Lord will do their utmost to obey his commandments and their lives will reflect a desire to honor God.

When we meet people like this and our desire is also to obey his Word, our decisions will complement each other's, and a friendship will be natural. As we strive to serve the Lord, it will become evident that this is better accomplished in the company of other brothers and sisters with the same heart and mind. Camaraderie is born out of sharing a common goal—especially when that goal ties us together as family under Christ.

*How do you feel when you meet someone new
and discover they love the Lord like you do?*

In a Crowd

When he saw the crowds, he had compassion on them,
because they were harassed and helpless,
like sheep without a shepherd.

MATTHEW 9:36 NIV

Just like a good father and a caring shepherd, when the Lord sees us lost and confused it fills him with compassion. He does not chastise us for our inadequacies but chooses to show us grace. He is not angry because we cannot find our own way; he steps in to lead us. His kind heart is full of mercy as he tirelessly pursues us. We were so desperate for salvation that he actually left heaven to come and redeem us. Since then, he continues to rescue us, often leaving the well-cared-for flock to search for each one of us who wanders off and becomes lost.

Jesus never abandons us to our hopeless wanderings but will go any length to intervene on our behalf. He mediates between heaven and earth, having lived in both, and is the only one who could bridge the gap. His is the only way that leads to eternal life! May we be instrumental in the lives of others as he uses us to extend his message of love and eternal life.

Do you have compassion on others who are engulfed in their sin?
Have you asked the Lord to fill you
with more compassion for his lost people?

Pedestals

> "Render true judgments, show kindness and mercy to one another, do not oppress the widow, the fatherless, the sojourner, or the poor, and let none of you devise evil against another in your heart."
>
> ZECHARIAH 7:9-10 ESV

Children of God have no business meddling in evil affairs. Since all our provisions come from God, there is no reason for us to cheat anyone else or submit inaccurate accounts. Kindness and mercy should be the default reaction of every Christian because of the grace we have been shown, and we should devise plans to do good for one another.

The Lord has a tender spot in his heart for the helpless and the disadvantaged. This may be someone who has lost their spouse and is reliant on one income or it could be someone who does not have the support of parents. It is perhaps a foreigner who is immersed in a culture that is not their own, or someone who feels marginalized from society. Most certainly, it includes the poor. These are the people we should run to with love and kindness. We should be quick to offer support and slow to judge.

Who needs your support and love?
Can you and your spouse do something together to help them?

Burdens Lifted

You should rather turn to forgive and comfort him,
or he may be overwhelmed by excessive sorrow.
2 CORINTHIANS 2:7 ESV

Marriage brings times of extreme happiness and joy, but it also sees times that require comfort and understanding. Having a spouse means you have someone sharing good and bad times. When something wonderful happens in your life, having someone to do the happy dance with is a blessing. Your love connects you in a way that makes you feel that every joy is a shared dream.

Your spouse also provides comfort. When you have a bad day and feel overwhelmed, just sharing those feelings lightens the load. Your spouse is the person in this world who loves you more than anyone else. Naturally, he or she is the person from whom you would seek comfort.

*Have you recently shared an accomplishment with your spouse?
Has there been a time when you needed comfort
and your spouse provided it?
Take time to thank each other today.*

Futile Flattery

May the LORD cut off all flattering lips,
The tongue that speaks great things.
PSALM 12:3 NASB

Communication between two or more individuals has great potential, because our tongue is one of our most powerful weapons. People who have spoken great things are those who believe that this weapon is their savior. For this reason, the psalmist prays for God to not only silence their arrogant, great words, but to take away their pompous source of communication. To begin with, this passage warns us of how despicable flattery and proud words are. Further, it shows that we must give an account for our words to the Lord.

We can use our communication to build up those around us. Our spouses and parents will probably all tell us that the words we speak have a tremendous impact on them. News outlets testify that a reporter's words impact those far beyond their social circle. Imagine the incredible impact we could have if flattering lips and the tongue that speaks great things would cease to exist in the church at large. We need to pray that our voices would speak the words of Christ instead of the natural responses that are typical for this world. Use your words and your influence to speak life into the heart of a hurting world.

Do you control your words or does your tongue control you?

Comfort in Suffering

If we have troubles, it is for your comfort and salvation, and if we have comfort, you also have comfort. This helps you to accept patiently the same sufferings we have. Our hope for you is strong, knowing that you share in our sufferings and also in the comfort we receive.

2 CORINTHIANS 1:6-7 NCV

The believers in Corinth were having a difficult time assessing why if Paul was truly an apostle, he would continually undergo such suffering. Wouldn't God spare him if he approved of what he was doing? What they did not yet understand was that suffering serves an important purpose. We learn a lot about Christ through suffering. We remember the importance of the Gospel message and its eternal promises, and we garner attention for our messages when we suffer.

It is not necessary that we go looking for suffering; the message of the Gospel attracts opposition naturally. We have a real enemy who attempts to thwart our plans, but when we suffer it becomes obvious to all that we sincerely believe in and will fight for the truth we live by. Believers are not exempt from suffering. What we are promised is that the Lord will always be with us to comfort and to guide us.

How has God comforted you through suffering and used it to teach you more about his abounding grace?

Soldiers Together

Put on every piece of God's armor so you will be able to resist the enemy in the time of evil. Then after the battle you will still be standing firm.

EPHESIANS 6:13 NLT

The battle is big, but Christians are equipped. Gazing around our world today, it is easy to feel overwhelmed, angry, scared, and drowned out. So many confused voices shout misguided idioms, so much contradictory information is pushed in our faces, and self-worship abounds. When we steal away from the world and find a quiet moment to soak in the Word of God, we remember again that we are never alone.

The Lord goes before us. He trains us and does not leave us defenseless. Everything we require for a life of victory has already been given to us. As we carefully consider each piece of armor the Lord has laid before us, it becomes apparent that it is the enemy who should cower in fear. Those who stand with God are on the winning side; we will be standing firm when the battle is finally over.

Have you adorned yourself with each piece of armor according to Ephesians 6?

Pure Ingredients

Clothe yourselves with the Lord Jesus Christ,
and do not think about how to gratify the desires of the flesh.

ROMANS 13:14 NIV

We are no longer slaves of sin, and we have no part in the deeds of darkness. The immoral acts Paul is referring to are listed in the previous verse: carousing, drunkenness, sexual immorality, debauchery, dissension, and jealousy. All these shameful stunts exist only to satisfy the urges of the flesh. Their focus is self-gratification, not love of God and others. If we are fixated on feeling good and doing whatever we want in the moment, we are worshipping ourselves and not God.

As children of light pulled out of the darkness, we have been instructed to clothe ourselves with Christ. This means we are to cast off the appearance of sin and darkness and take on his image. We live like he lived and think about how we can honor him. Although it is not our purpose or motivation, obedience to God is always rewarded, and it leads to far more satisfaction, contentment, and joy than a life lived in pursuit of our own agendas ever could.

When you think about how you could please God
instead of yourself, what comes to mind?
As an immediate practical example,
how can you please your spouse before focusing on yourself?

God's Riches

"You cannot serve both God and money."
MATTHEW 6:24 NIV

The systems and mentality of the world contradict the laws of God. The former promotes seeking our own happiness and living for ourselves, whereas the latter commands that we seek to honor God and look out for the welfare of others. Money and material wealth can be used as tools in service to the Lord, but if earthly riches and fame captivate us and steal our devotion, it is displeasing to God and devastating to our souls.

The Lord will not stand as second in command, and we cannot serve him if we are serving ourselves. God desires to be our one and only master. He rules in love and all his ways are just. He has guaranteed us eternal life, peace, joy, and a family with him forever. His love for us is everlasting and unparalleled. It is foolish to throw this all aside in pursuit of any lesser master.

What is the difference between
owning wealth and wealth owning you?
How do you and your spouse encourage each other
to remain wise in the area of finance?

Sacrificial Love

You adulterers! Don't you realize that friendship with the world makes you an enemy of God? I say it again: If you want to be a friend of the world, you make yourself an enemy of God.

JAMES 4:4 NLT

When it comes to the subject of submission to God, James leaves no room to question how serious a matter it is. God desires to be the first and only King in our lives. He did, after all, create us, save us, and now sustains us. We owe him everything and especially our allegiance. When we place anything above him, James likens it to someone having an affair. Once we have promised our loyalty to our spouse, breaking that bond with someone else is very damaging.

When we forsake God for anything or anyone else, it hurts his heart. He is a good and loving God who is willing to accept us back if we repent and turn away from our wicked choices, but disloyalty is never a worthwhile choice to begin with. It is a difficult road back once we start down it because sin has a way of pulling us along and alluring us toward death. It is far wiser to keep our eyes fixed on God from the start.

Maintaining loyalty is difficult with God and with our spouses. What are you doing in your life to fight off the snares of the devil and keep your commitments to God and your spouse?

Price of Wealth

Better is the little of the righteous
than the abundance of many wicked.
PSALM 37:16 NASB

The abundance of the wicked may seem tantalizing to those of us who have very little, but meager wages earned honestly are of far greater value in terms of what truly matters. To gain wealth through evil means is worthless because the days of the wicked are numbered. Whether the Lord has blessed the righteous with great wealth or taught them to endure with limited rations, we are instructed to offer what we have to God and find contentment in his love.

This life and its treasures will all fade away one day, so it would be foolish to trade our souls for comfortable living here and now. The Lord seeks to increase our faith. All the pleasures of this life pale in comparison to a life lived serving him; for true joy can only be found in him. He is both our purpose and our pleasure.

*What do you and your spouse have
that can be used to serve God?*

Supporting Role

He who heeds discipline shows the way to life,
but whoever ignores correction leads others astray.

PROVERBS 10:17 NIV

The decisions we make, whether negative or positive, affect not only us but others in our lives. Hate and love both have a multiplying effect, and the choices we make always carry repercussions. The Lord disciplines those he loves because he cares about our development and our maturity. If we are humble enough to receive his loving discipline and grow from it, we can use these lessons, and the wisdom they have taught us, to bless others.

Having a faith that we can share is an incredible privilege. If we live contrary to God's ordinances and are unwilling to learn or yield, it is to our detriment and the detriment of others. We can be a blessing or a hinderance to our spouses, family, friends, or others we may have an influence on. This is especially true with leaders in the church, teachers, and parents. Keep other people who are susceptible or young in the faith in mind when you are choosing which course to take.

How do you react to correction from your spouse?

Finding Flaws

"In the same way you judge others, you will be judged,
and with the measure you use, it will be measured to you."

MATTHEW 7:2 NIV

Critique and criticism are two words with the same root but very different meanings. A critique is a detailed analysis of something. But a criticism highlights the faults in people and their actions. Criticism can kill a marriage.

Two imperfect people are going to have flaws and fights. But criticizing one another doesn't solve any problems. A critical person is actually one who lacks communication skills. If you have an issue you want to address, don't attack your spouse's character. Instead, address how a particular behavior makes you feel. And if your mate comes to you with a problem, listen with an open mind. You'll both be happier for it.

Is there an area in your marriage where you feel criticized?
How can you work to communicate better?

A New Worldview

Suppose someone comes into your church meeting wearing nice clothes
and a gold ring. At the same time a poor person comes in wearing old,
dirty clothes. You show special attention to the one wearing nice clothes
and say, "Please, sit here in this good seat." But you say to the poor person,
"Stand over there," or, "Sit on the floor by my feet." What are you doing?
You are making some people more important than others, and with evil
thoughts you are deciding that one person is better.

JAMES 2:2-4 NCV

*M*arriage joins two households and two backgrounds. You may
have grown up in a family that was very open and loving, while
your spouse grew up in a home that looked at others by different
standards. Merging two conflicting viewpoints means establishing a
new way of relating to others.

Often, the way we look at others is personality-related. Some
personalities find it easier to love everyone, while others are more
closed off. As you learn how to live with each other based on your
backgrounds, personalities, and other factors, remember that God's
love within both of you should be the filter through which you view
the world.

Do you see any prejudices in your lives as a couple?
What can you do to overcome them?

Submit in Love

Submit to one another
out of reverence for Christ.
EPHESIANS 5:21 NIV

Submission does not involve passively following what everyone else says or does. To submit within the context of its use in Scripture entails putting the needs of others above our own. We can do this because of our reverence for Christ and because we see how he put our needs before his own wellbeing. Jesus not only put our lives above his, he called us to do likewise and promised to take care of all our needs.

We have an example to follow and an assurance that he will always be with us, ready to catch us and care for us. Within the bond of marriage, the Bible is very clear that we are to submit to each other and put the needs of our spouses above our own. This provides a clear picture of Christ's love to anyone privy to the union, and it also creates harmony and safety for both husband and wife.

How can you choose to put your spouse first today?

Devoted in Love

God, being rich in mercy, because of the great love with which he loved us,
even when we were dead in our trespasses, made us alive together with
Christ—by grace you have been saved—and raised us up with him and
seated us with him in the heavenly places in Christ Jesus, so that in the
coming ages he might show the immeasurable riches of his grace in kindness
toward us in Christ Jesus.

EPHESIANS 2:4-7 ESV

There is an important distinction between salvation and sanctification. The former is the work Christ did on the cross to save us from the death penalty our sins deserved. The latter is the work the Holy Spirit continues to do in us as we grow in grace and in relationship with God. The point at which we began our journey was lost and without grace. The Lord rescued us and filled us with hope and peace. It is by his merit alone that we have life everlasting!

As we engage with others who are still misguided in thinking they can achieve their own salvation, we need to remember that we are no more deserving than they of the grace our God freely bestowed upon us. Because of the kindness and love we have been shown, we can freely give the same kindness and love to those who are rude and hateful toward us. Never forget the dark place God pulled you out of or the lavish gifts he so readily blessed you with. Give love to others based on what you have received, not based on what they deserve.

What has God specifically given you
that you can use to bless your spouse?

Blessed by Trust

His pleasure is not in the strength of the horse,
nor his delight in the legs of the warrior;
the LORD delights in those who fear him,
who put their hope in his unfailing love.

PSALM 147:10-11 NIV

*O*ur demonstrations of power and might do not impress the Lord. He wants us to learn how to trust in him and rely on his strength, rather than attempt to muscle our way through life by our own means and willpower. Humility is far more pleasing to the Lord than ability. Our skills and strength are gifts from him, and humble love is our grateful gift back to him.

The mighty horse and the tender butterfly were both created by God and are both cared for by him. Furthermore, both animals also reflect a separate side of his character; he holds all the power in the universe, and yet also holds us gently in his embrace. Even if we feel confident and capable, we ought to fear God and continue to follow his leadership. This will be pleasing to him and will keep us out of a lot of potential trouble.

Is God's strength the security you run to,
or do you depend on your own achievements?

Celebrating Success

I was constantly at his side.
I was filled with delight day after day,
rejoicing always in his presence,
rejoicing in his whole world and delighting in mankind.

PROVERBS 8:30-31 NIV

These are the words of Wisdom, personified, speaking about the creation of the world. Earlier in the chapter, Wisdom identified that she was the first of God's works. Why was Wisdom constantly at God's side? She was filled with delight day after day. From this passage we learn that the whole of creation was made through and interlaced with Wisdom herself. We live in a world of perfect logic. This is a cosmos, operating with seamless order and natural repeatability. Our beautiful surroundings are not chaotic, unpredictable, and unplanned. Instead we are daily witnesses to the intrinsic wisdom that entwines itself within everything.

Can we see God's wisdom around us? In the midst of our packed schedules and difficult relationships, do we recognize the order in the universe, the fact that God created our world to be good and perfect for us? Despite the fall of creation, God's fingerprint remains prominently across the earth. The question for us is whether we will join in rejoicing in his whole world and delighting in mankind.

How do the wonders of nature declare the glory of God?
What are some specific examples?

February

Don't owe anything to anyone, except your
outstanding debt to continually love one another,
for the one who learns to love has fulfilled every
requirement of the law.

ROMANS 13:8 TPT

A Reliable Partner

"The LORD, the LORD, the compassionate and gracious God,
slow to anger, abounding in love and faithfulness."
EXODUS 34:6 NIV

Reliability is an important trait for any couple. There's vast security in having someone who sticks with you. We experience perfect reliability with God, and from him we can learn qualities that will enhance our marriages. The first is compassion: caring about what touches the heart of our spouse. There is graciousness, the ability to dispense mercy when needed. A slow response to anger is another important trait that will benefit our relationships. Step back and take a deep breath when needed, but don't lash out in anger.

The final two traits that God shares with us in this verse are love and faithfulness. Those vows we took on our wedding day "to love and to cherish," and "until death do us part," were real promises. Let us also vow to always be the one our sweetheart can depend on, no matter what situation arises.

Do you feel secure in your marriage?
What traits do you need to improve
so that your spouse can depend on you?

Sound Wisdom

With him are strength and sound wisdom;
the deceived and the deceiver are his.

JOB 12:16 ESV

*D*eceit runs rampant and leads many people astray. Our human wisdom will fail because there will always be someone smarter or more articulate. Our sense of right and wrong, true and false, good and bad must stem from the Scriptures and a knowledge of the Holy One. Job's friends preached that he suffered because of sin, but Job was sure of his innocence.

We do not always know what God is doing, but we can recognize truth from the lies. Suffering is not a sign of sin. When we suffer and still abstain from sinning, it pleases God's heart. None of us will be exempt from pain in this life since tragedy befalls the unjust and the just. One day, God will wipe away our tears, fill our hearts with laughter, and reward our obedience. We cannot judge his pleasure by our success, only by what his Word teaches us.

What benefits have you seen come out of your suffering?

Light and Dark

What fellowship can light have with darkness?
2 CORINTHIANS 6:14 NIV

When light moves into darkness, the darkness disappears. Paul is not warning us to stay away from the darkness, but he is pointing out that the two do not coexist. Darkness also cannot overcome the light. We should be careful about entering into any close relationship with someone who is not walking in the light because they will not share the same values. We are not walking the same way, nor toward the same end goal.

To be yoked with darkness means constant tugging and tension since our directions will differ. Aside from influencing relationships, we should not avoid the darkness, but carry our light into it. The light of Christ within us is powerful enough to illuminate the most evil places. We should make sure that we are having a positive impact on the world, rather than it having a negative impact on us.

How can you and your spouse maintain light
when you are surrounded by darkness?

The One

Behold, God is my salvation,
I will trust and not be afraid;
For the LORD God is my strength and my song,
And He has become my salvation.

ISAIAH 12:2 NASB

There is something satisfied in a soul that is rescued from the brink of death. God is our salvation. He is the one who saves us from hopelessness, like a blessed vessel in a shoreless ocean. After he saves us, our soul yields all trust, forsaking earthly fear and clinging to him closely. Never have we been so safe. How can pharisaical religion result from this? What a horrific life must we be living if we pretend to love God.

It sounds strange, but most of us experience a time when religion seems boring. These times of apathy can be broken by passages like the one above. Isaiah says that the Lord God is not only our strength, but our song. Our hearts are filled with a symphony that is the Lord's love. Oh God, please help us to abandon every insincere emotion as we rejoice in your salvation.

When your walk with God begins to feel dull,
or when your spouse's does, how can you
encourage each other to rediscover God's goodness?

Self-Control

A man without self-control is like
a city broken into and left without walls.
PROVERBS 25:28 ESV

When sailing a boat, one needs a sail, a rudder, and a good breeze. Imagine trying to sail to a particular destination by relying only on the wind to get there, with no way to steer. Sometimes the wind blows one way, then another, and sometimes not at all. You can't depend on it.

Trying to steer your marriage based on emotion creates the same problem. Emotion is like the wind. Sometimes you're up, sometimes down, and sometimes you're indifferent. Trying to reach a particular destination in your relationship by relying solely on emotion is nearly impossible. God is the most reliable rudder for your marriage, so let him guide you safely to shore. Don't get caught out on the water in the middle of a storm without him.

*What are some areas where you struggle with
allowing emotion to control you in your marriage?*

Uprooting Bitterness

In your anger do not sin.
Do not let the sun go down while you are still angry,
and do not give the devil a foothold.
EPHESIANS 4:26-27 ESV

Most of us began our newlywed days with starry-eyed visions of future, euphoric days. Indeed, many days are full of joy, but there are also days of rip-roaring anger, where steam rises from our ears. Sometimes, it is an important problem, but often the silliest issues set us off. Anger can be deadly in a marriage if we let it take root, and we allow bitterness to set in.

God cautions us against bitterness when he tells us to patch up divisions before the sun goes down. He knows that anger festers and grows when we don't deal with it, and that allows the devil to creep into our marriages, creating discord in a holy union that God put together. The words "I'm sorry," and, "I was wrong; will you forgive me?" are sometimes hard to say, but they are invaluable in protecting and preserving our homes and marriages.

What's the best way to handle anger?
Do you have trouble forgiving each other
when you've made each other angry?

Life and Peace

If people's thinking is controlled by the sinful self, there is death.
But if their thinking is controlled by the Spirit, there is life and peace.

ROMANS 8:6 NCV

God is King and he does not share his crown. We may choose to serve him or serve ourselves. He has offered us a better way, a higher road, one which leads to life and peace. Being ruled by our own sinful thinking and indulgences leads to death. Sin is attractive and deceiving; it often promises things it can't deliver. The further down that road of lies we travel, the more difficult it is to redirect and walk toward the truth. Difficult—but not impossible.

It may involve some backtracking, but the Spirit of God is there to guide us. The more we dwell on goodness and the things of God, the more the Spirit helps us overcome our old mindsets and clears out the lies. The road of righteousness that leads to life is difficult but simple: we must deny ourselves and submit to God's better way.

What do you think about most throughout your day?
Who do you seek to please: God or yourself?

Absolute Peace

Perfect, absolute peace surrounds those
whose imaginations are consumed with you;
they confidently trust in you.

ISAIAH 26:3 TPT

Being steadfast is not easy. It is not zeal, inspired by extreme passion. It is not a dull perseverance. It is the quality of a watchman who not only stays awake but also scans the horizon, actively employing his gaze. God calls for our minds to be steadfast, promising us peace in return. More than that, it is a perfect peace, like that hinted at in Philippians 4:7 which passes all understanding.

In difficult occupations and responsibilities, it becomes easy to give up on active thinking and instead live on autopilot in order to escape stressful situations. Many people cope this way. God knows that resisting the urge to be complacent is difficult. He feels our burden when we seek for mental fortitude against temptation and hopelessness. He can see that we only remain steadfast by trusting in him. In light of this, Christ will bring the steadfast of mind into his perfect peace.

When you disengage your mind,
where does your imagination go?

Unfolding

*The unfolding of your words gives light;
it gives understanding to the simple.*

PSALM 119:130 NASB

*H*ave you and your spouse ever been in a situation where you didn't know what to do? You struggled with the decision. You agonized over it. And then a loving friend said, "Well, if you did… then all of the pieces would fall into place." And suddenly, their wise words made an impossible situation become possible.

It's much like being in a dark room during a power outage. You can't see where the furniture is or if there are things on the floor that will trip you. But when the lights come back on, you see clearly. That's what this verse depicts. When God says something to us, it's like having light come into a dark room—and it's so clear and simple that everyone can understand it. Do you and your spouse need to understand what to do in a situation? Ask God to put his spotlight on the words he has for you.

*Can you think of a time when God has helped you
through his Word to understand what to do in a situation?
How did that cast light on the solution?*

Preserved

Love the LORD, all you his saints!
The LORD preserves the faithful
but abundantly repays the one who acts in pride.

PSALM 31:23 ESV

The Lord is faithful to a standard of morality. If you remain faithful to God, he will preserve you as his own. Simultaneously, the pride of a seeming philanthropist will not be overlooked by the Almighty. He must consider every deed and every thought. We cannot be one of his saints by our own deeds, but by Christ's deeds we may be counted as his own and thus preserved from wrath. It would be far worse if our God were arbitrary in his judgment.

The psalmist may have known some subjective rulers and the unpredictable, inconsistent judgments they pass. With full praise we rejoice because our God has promised to preserve the faithful and also to abundantly repay the one who acts in pride. If we know that Christ has washed us clean, there is no fear that God will condemn us. Once we have become his godly ones, we are unequivocally preserved.

Why does God hate pride?
What does a proud person actually believe?

Comfort Zone

As He was going along by the Sea of Galilee, He saw Simon and Andrew, the brother of Simon, casting a net in the sea; for they were fishermen. And Jesus said to them, "Follow Me, and I will make you become fishers of men." Immediately they left their nets and followed him.

MARK 1:16-18 NASB

Some of us enter marriage with the hope that we're going to set down deep roots. We crave constancy and its security, and there's nothing wrong with that. However, it usually doesn't take long for us to discover that life and marriage are full of changes. If we're going to deal well with that, we have to be flexible—especially when it comes to serving God.

Sometimes, God asks us to be flexible, perhaps to leave our comfort zones or give up a dream that we've had on our hearts. His dreams are always bigger and better, and it builds an amazing bond in a marriage when we are flexible enough to follow God as a couple.

How can you and your spouse
be more flexible about serving God?
Can you think of a time or two when he changed your plans?
How did that affect your marriage?

Safe and Sound

When you lie down, you will not be afraid;
When you lie down, your sleep will be sweet.
Do not be afraid of sudden fear
Nor of the onslaught of the wicked when it comes.

PROVERBS 3:24-25 NASB

When our conscience is guilt-free, it is far easier to sleep at night. We also know that our safety comes from God and we can find rest in that promise. Peter slept soundly in prison, even though he was supposed to be executed the following morning, because he trusted the Lord with his soul. It is simple rational that by avoiding sin, we also avoid the consequences of sin.

Following God is not a backdoor escape from all trouble, but it does stand to reason that we forgo a lot of unnecessary headaches and hardships when we decide to trust God and do what he says. Those who follow God are still subject to a lot of evil in this world, but we do not need to fear because even if our bodies are destroyed, our souls are safe and sound with our Savior. It is the wicked who should fear because they must answer a righteous God for their life decisions.

Do you sleep peacefully at night, or do your actions haunt you?

Heart at Rest

God is your confidence in times of crisis,
keeping your heart at rest in every situation.
PROVERBS 3:26 TPT

We do not live as the rest of the world lives. When crisis hits, we remain unshaken because our confidence comes from God. If our confidence was in our own strength, we could be overthrown. If it was in another human, we would be met with disappointment. If we are trusting in the systems erected in this world, we will soon discover that we are out of place in this world because we live for an eternal kingdom.

We must place our assurance and find our rest in God and him alone because that is the only firm foundation. No catastrophe or crippling condition can cause us to lose heart when it is God who holds us together. In every horrifying situation, we will stand in contrast to the crowd because our hearts are at rest. We will not act in fear because our minds are at peace. We know the Lord will guide us and keep us safe. He is more than just a King; he is also an involved and loving Father who covers us with his peace and fills us with confidence.

In the midst of crisis, what truths can you remind yourself of?

Everyday Sweetness

A person finds joy in giving an apt reply—
and how good is a timely word!

PROVERBS 15:23 NIV

Valentine's Day is a time for giving flowers or heart-shaped boxes of chocolates, but often it's the carefully chosen words in a card or a hand-written love note that mean the most. This day for sweethearts gives us a chance to express our love and our appreciation and to say the things that often go unsaid.

It's also a time to reflect on how God joins two lives together in marriage, giving thanks for the relationship that makes us complete as a couple. Wise couples take advantage of Valentine's Day, but they also carry that sweetness into the following days. We don't have to buy gifts on a daily basis, but we can share the gift of our words— heartfelt thoughts that will touch the soul of our God-given spouse.

What words can you use to encourage and uplift your spouse?
What words do you need to hear most?

Enduring Love

Give thanks to the LORD, for he is good;
his love endures forever.

PSALM 118:1 NIV

Most wedding vows include some type of forever phrase, and all imply that the pledge we make to our spouses is binding. Once we commit ourselves to someone in marriage, the expectation is that we will keep our promises. God's everlasting love is a perfect promise. Once he enters our lives, we are his forever. We sin and we make mistakes, but his love for us never wavers. Thanks to Christ's sacrifice, he looks at us as if we never got off the path and loves us just the same.

Married love should be the same way. We love our spouses because they are God's gift to us. We know from the beginning that our mates are not perfect. However, we also love them with a forever love—a love that grows, forgives, and endures. In our wedding vows, we promised forever love, and with God's help, we can keep that promise.

Have you talked about the forever love that you share?
Thank each other for times when love endured difficulty.

Benefits of Generosity

He brought me to the banqueting house,
and his banner over me was love.

SONG OF SOLOMON 2:4 ESV

*M*arching soldiers would raise banners over their armies with the names of their kings or leaders written on them. When King Solomon wrote that the banner flying over him was the Lord's and on it was inscribed "Love," he was declaring two things: that he was a soldier in the army of the Lord, and that God was love. He wanted his readers to know without any doubt that his allegiance was to the God of love.

God is more than just loving; he is love himself. Love originated with him; he is the author of it. The love we share in marriage is a glimmer of the love the Father feels for us. The more we learn about his incredible love, the deeper we can feel love and the wider we are able to share it. To truly love our spouses the best we possibly can, we must first get to know Love himself.

If your allegiance is to God,
how will that be evident to others who know you,
including your spouse?

Trusting Together

Those who know the LORD trust him,
because he will not leave those who come to him.

PSALM 9:10 NCV

Every couple faces challenges. They may be about our health, jobs, or relationships. Some problems are financial; some of our dilemmas are caused by time or the lack of it. Our biggest problem when we face life's challenges is that we think we need to solve them on our own. You are a team that God has joined together. Together you face times of trouble. And together you can support each other and pray together.

The Lord has promised not to abandon those who seek him. In prayer, you may receive revelations that will help overcome obstacles, or you may not obtain the solution you seek. Healing may not be the answer, a new job may or may not appear, but rest in the knowledge that the Lord knows you, loves you, and has your best at heart. Trusting God together will strengthen your faith.

Do you go to God together in prayer when facing life's obstacles?
What is the biggest challenge each of you face right now?
Can you trust the Lord to handle problems?

Giving Cheerfully

You must each decide in your heart how much to give.
And don't give reluctantly or in response to pressure.
"For God loves a person who gives cheerfully."

2 CORINTHIANS 9:7 NLT

God is not lacking in resources; he has all the power and wealth in the universe. It is our honor to be able to give back to him what he has entrusted to us. Our whole lives ought to be subject to his rule, but when we give from our finances, we declare that money is not where we find our security. We also demonstrate compassion and unity with other members of the body of Christ, whether we are giving to the church, a missionary, or someone in need.

There are other ways we can give too. We can offer our time, talents, wisdom, or possessions. Whatever we decide to give, it should be an individual choice determined by what God has laid on our hearts. Giving is such a blessed act of faith, it should fill us with joy and cheer! The Lord does not want begrudging gifts or excess earnings, he wants our hearts and full surrender. He can grow amazing wonders out of the small seeds we offer him.

Do you and your spouse have a system set up for giving?
How do you decide together what to give and to whom?

Sharing Difficulties

May the righteous be glad and rejoice before God;
may they be happy and joyful.
PSALM 68:3 NIV

Are we worried about nothing? Are we redeemed, yet still under the weight of regret? Maybe our life is simply boring or inundated with temporal concerns. Psalm 68 insists that the righteous ought to be glad. There is no other posture in times of peace. It is strange that we can be righteous before God, purchased by the Son's blood, yet neglect to find joy in our lives. What else could be more rewarding or more desirable?

We are righteous before God, redeemed and free, given the command to rejoice. If any of Christ's commands were light and easy, it is this one. Insincere happiness is a heavy burden. God hopes for us to rejoice with gladness of heart, not just out of obligation. God's character is conducive to our enjoyment, and to our exultation, which makes this command all the more rational. In light of what Christ has done, we can allow the realization of his incredible salvation to fill us with joy.

How do you and your spouse practice being joyful?

Right Jealousy

*I am jealous for you with the jealousy of God himself.
I promised you as a pure bride to one husband—Christ.*

2 CORINTHIANS 11:2 NLT

In the days of Paul, engagement and marriage were enacted quite differently than they are today. A father would betroth his daughter to her future husband months and sometimes years in advance, and then he would have a personal responsibility to protect his daughter's purity until the union was made. Paul used this understood cultural practice as an analogy for how he felt regarding the church in Corinth. Since Paul founded, grew, and taught the church, he felt like he was a spiritual father to it. His heart was invested in its well-being and he cared about the people deeply.

The early Christians, like us today, had been promised to Christ. They were his beloved even though they were not yet with him in his heavenly home. False teachers had begun to creep up, proclaiming a different message and drawing the Corinthian Christians away from following Jesus. Understandably, Paul was concerned for their loyalty and was committed to helping them stay on the right path. His jealously pursued them for the sake of Christ and for their own salvation.

If you are betrothed to Christ, how should you be acting?

Know-It-All

Live in harmony with each other.
Don't be too proud to enjoy the company of ordinary people.
And don't think you know it all!

ROMANS 12:16 NLT

If Christ, who was the fullness of God, was willing to come to this earth and submit himself to the company of humans, then we have no excuse to disassociate anyone because we perceive them to be less than ourselves. One of the revolutionary aspects of the early Christian church was how inclusive it was toward women, foreigners, slaves, the uneducated, prostitutes, lepers, and anyone else.

We have all come from different places with separate struggles. God has welcomed with open arms anyone humble enough to accept his message. Until all has been revealed, there will continue to be disagreements within the body of Christ. These are inevitable, but they also provide us with the opportunity to exercise humility. Paul is not instructing us to avoid differences of opinion or all think the same way, but he is teaching us that we ought to fine tune our words and actions to be harmonious with other people. We can all learn from each other if we are not too proud. None of us has all the answers.

Is there anyone in your life who believes differently than you?
How do you associate melodically
without compromising your convictions?

Mind Reading

Have unity of mind, sympathy, brotherly love,
a tender heart, and a humble mind.
1 PETER 3:8 ESV

Having previously addressed separate groups within the body of Christ (wives, husbands, slaves), Peter now summarizes five overarching commandments applicable to all people. Christians are to have unity of mind with regards to the teaching of Jesus. His words are what continue to unite us across all generations and far reaches of the world. We are also to be sympathetic to the needs of others. It is not enough to only care about our individual standing before God. Since we are collectively members of a greater body of believers, we are to treat others as if they were part of our own body and express active compassion for them.

To have brotherly love for one another further clarifies the perspective we are intended to have as members of the family of God. Displaying a tender heart means more than simply sympathy; we are moved to respond. Our hearts are tender toward the hurts and needs of others and not suspicious, judgmental, or calloused. All of these are much easier if we have a humble mind. Our motivation is not our own glorification but to glorify God. We can do that by loving and supporting his people just as he taught us to do.

What do each of these five traits look like when lived out?

Open Your Pantry

He who supplies seed to the sower and bread for food will also supply
and increase your store of seed and will enlarge the harvest of your
righteousness. You will be enriched in every way so that you can be
generous on every occasion, and through us your generosity will result
in thanksgiving to God.

2 CORINTHIANS 9:10-11 NIV

We have a duty to one another. How can we expect to receive
mercy from God whilst withholding grace from each other? Our
Father loves us deeply and has given us many blessings. In turn, we
ought to share what we have with his other children whom he also
loves. This is the greatest way we can thank him for his generosity
toward us.

As Christians, we do not need to stockpile or hoard worldly goods
since we understand that it is God who supplies for our needs. Of
course, we should be wise, thrifty, and perceptive of the days to
come, but not to the extent that it replaces charity and hospitality.
If we truly want to worship God and show him love, then we are to
serve others and attend to their needs. That is what he has asked his
followers to do.

*What is the difference between wisely saving for the future
and being greedy?*

Pure Religion

Pure and undefiled religion in the sight of our God and Father is this:
to visit orphans and widows in their distress,
and to keep oneself unstained by the world.

JAMES 1:27 NASB

*O*ver and over Jesus emphasized that he was not impressed by religiosity or ceremonies exalting pious performances. He preached love. He taught humility. He lived selflessly. Furthermore, he expects his followers to do likewise. Assisting those in need is far more precious in the sight of God than legalistically maintaining an image of devout Christianity.

Keeping unstained by the world does not mean avoiding others who we feel are less virtuous than ourselves. It is cautioning us away from following the world's systems, which are built on a framework of self-gratification and individual promotion. If our eyes are fixed on our own goals and aspirations, we will likely miss the plights of those around us who are in distress. As Christians, we are not to become so self-absorbed, pursuing the world's version of success, that we lose sight of our true calling which is to be the hands and feet of Christ

Who do you know in distress?
How can you love that person this week
the way Jesus taught you to?

Tithing Time

Suppose someone has enough to live and sees a brother or sister in need, but does not help. Then God's love is not living in that person.

1 JOHN 3:17 NCV

Following the money trail is a good way to expose a person's heart and true motivation. Obviously, God does not need our money, but instead of addressing all the needs of his people he invites us to participate with him. We have been given an opportunity to love others as ambassadors of God. Are we stingy with our wealth and possessions—the very wealth assets God entrusted to us to begin with? That reveals the place our hearts are; caring more for our own preservation and comfort than for our brothers and sisters.

Are we generous with what we have been blessed with? Giving to others displays gratitude for what we have been given, trust in God to supply for all our needs, and an active love for others, which is the Gospel message. God has promised to take care of us, so we ought to care for one another. We find our comfort in his promises not in financial security or worldly pleasures.

Who is in need today?
What do they need?
How can you love them?

Supporting Others

We who are strong ought to bear with the failings of the weak
and not to please ourselves.

ROMANS 15:1 NIV

The Lord did not grant us freedom from the law so we could use it
to indulge in our own desires, but so we could proclaim his freedom
to those still stuck in captivity. Everyone is on their own walk with
the Lord and at varying levels of maturity. It is not for us to judge,
but to love them and support their walk. Even after accepting
Christ's salvation, many Christians do not understand the full extent
of the forgiveness and freedom they have been given. It is Christ
who makes us pure, Christ who sanctifies us, and Christ who bears
our weaknesses.

When someone weaker in the faith is caught up in the letter of
the law rather than the love of Christ, our response should be
to show them the love of Christ. God does not require complete
understanding and maturity from us immediately because he
understands that sanctification is a process. It is important that we
allow others the grace and time to come to a fuller understanding
of the love of God as they realize it over time. We can support them
through the process by laying our own liberties aside for the sake of
their conscience.

*What are some examples of freedoms
we have been given that cause others to stumble?
What is God calling you to lay aside for the sake of someone else?*

Honest Communication

Love does not delight in evil
but rejoices with the truth.

1 CORINTHIANS 13:6 NIV

Nothing drives a wedge between a husband and wife faster than dishonesty. In marriage, that could be unfaithfulness, untruths, half-truths, finances, and the like. Avoiding these can be much easier if your marriage relationship is based on truth and trust.

A truthful marriage is a healthy one, and we all want healthy marriages. If your marriage is not healthy, schedule regular sessions, alone or with a therapist, to discuss what is going on openly and honestly. Agree on rules for the discussion, such as no hurt feelings, no interrupting, just discussion with no defense, etc. Communication is an excellent way to practice truth in your marriage. It takes work, but it is well worth it.

Do you need to discuss areas of your marriage
with your spouse?
Set aside a few moments for that to happen now.

Walk in Light

If we claim to have fellowship with him
and yet walk in the darkness,
we lie and do not live out the truth.

1 JOHN 1:6 NIV

What's wrong with a little white lie? If a statement is not one hundred percent true, you may think it will not hurt anyone. Often the problem is not whether one lie will be hurtful, but the next one, or the next. Little white lies pile up. When you lie, you have to remember exactly what you said in order to keep the lie going. If you slip up, you may have to tell another lie to continue the first one, and suddenly there is little truth in your lie.

Honesty is always the best policy. When you tell the truth, there is no worry of tripping up later, but that is not the best reason to be truthful. God directed us to always be truthful, and that command extends to our marriages. Married couples living in an honest and truthful manner develop trusting relationships. When that bond is sure, they can also build trusting relationships with others, sharing God's love with them in truth.

Is your relationship a trusting one?
Share what is on your heart.
Have you shared the blessings
of a Christ-centered marriage with another couple?

March

An enemy might defeat one person,
but two people together can defend themselves;
a rope that is woven of three strings is hard to break.

ECCLESIASTES 4:12 NCV

Job's Heart

"Have you considered my servant Job? There is no one on earth like him;
he is blameless and upright, a man who fears God and shuns evil. And he
still maintains his integrity, though you incited me against him to ruin him
without any reason."

JOB 2:3 NIV

The Bible tells us that we will go through hard times in our lives,
and it's not always because we did something wrong or made a
mistake. Satan uses these times to try and break our spirits and tear
us down, but God uses them to give us a deeper relationship with
him. God's power is made manifest in our weaknesses. It's how he
shows us his might, and it underlines how much we need him. If we
were sufficient on our own, we would have no need for God to save
us, but we are sorely lacking. God allows our cup to be emptied so
he can fill it with his presence and love.

Job endured sickness, poverty, and the death of his loved ones
and still he glorified God even when his friends accused him of
wrongdoing and his wife told him to curse God. We should all work
toward having the kind of undying faith that Job exhibited amid his
extreme trials.

How do people see you react in difficult circumstances?
Is it glorifying to God?

Facing Trouble

The righteous person faces many troubles,
but the LORD comes to the rescue each time.

PSALM 34:19 NLT

Sometimes things go wrong and we are left wondering why. Despite our prayers and fasting, despite our service to the Lord, we still endure troubles and are faced with disappointments like everyone else. It has often been asked why bad things happen to good people. Why does God allow it to rain on the just and the unjust alike? King David's psalm offers encouragement for these times. Even though we face difficulties and afflictions, we can trust Yahweh to deliver us no matter the depth of the issue.

The children of God and those who have refused his grace all live together in a world full of evil. The difference, however, is with God on our side we have hope and a promise that he will always come through for us even on the tough days when it seems hope is lost. God is in charge and he will clear a path for us. It may seem like we are faced with a desperate situation, but we are not alone: the Word of God stands true for every occasion and every situation.

*What difficulty are you and your spouse facing right now
that you would like to pray for God's deliverance from?*

Inexplicable Joy

Though you have not seen him, you love him;
and even though you do not see him now,
you believe in him and are filled
with an inexpressible and glorious joy.

1 PETER 1:8 NIV

Peter walked with Jesus while he was on the earth. He knew him personally and had heard his words for himself. He found it noteworthy that God's elect people, who had been exiled and scattered afar, loved Jesus even though they had never seen him. Hearing his words preached and learning of his death and resurrection had filled them with inexplicable joy as they chose to put their faith in him.

It is rare that someone would die for someone else, and almost unheard of that anyone would be willing to die for a lie. An estimated two million Christians from the first 325 years after Christ's death clung to their faith in Christ Jesus and the message he came to bring and were murdered for it. These men and women were persecuted and martyred in unthinkable ways, yet they were overcome with a glorious joy! Even though they had never seen Jesus with their eyes, they had heard his life-giving words and knew that he was God. Their faith was stronger than even death.

How can you be sure that Jesus' words are true?

Difficult to Love

"Love your enemies! Do good to them. Lend to them without expecting
to be repaid. Then your reward from heaven will be very great, and you will
truly be acting as children of the Most High, for he is kind to those who are
unthankful and wicked."

LUKE 6:35 NLT

Human nature gravitates toward trade and reciprocity. If someone
does something for you, you are expected to do something for them.
If someone harms you, naturally you want to see them pay for it. In
this way we tend to seek out people who benefit us, so it is a strange
concept to consider when the Bible tells us to do good to people
who are our enemies. These people are downright harmful to our
self-interest and wellbeing. We are not inclined to cater to our own
downfall, so this is not a readily received message.

Instead of justifying our exemption from this mandate, we should
remember that the ways of the Lord are higher than our own,
and he is worthy of our surrender. For us to be like Christ and
overcome our human tendencies, we are invited to his standard of
love. He is kind to both good and evil people and he gives us all the
opportunity to join him in his eternal kingdom. We should love our
enemies because of the higher calling we have: to glorify the Lord
and keep our priorities on things which are eternal.

Are there people in your life who cause you harm?
How can you love them?

The Fruit Basket

"The fruit of the Spirit is love, joy, peace, forbearance,
kindness, goodness, faithfulness, gentleness and self-control.
Against such things there is no law."

GALATIANS 5:22-23 NIV

After having compiled a list of natural, wicked tendencies which stem from a life of someone following their own human desires, Paul offered an alternate list of what the fruit of a life devoted to God is. When the Spirit of God moves into our hearts, the core of our pursuits change from me focused to God focused. Naturally, our lives will look different as our choices resemble the true desires of our hearts.

The term *fruit* Paul chose to use here is not a plural term but singular. This means that all these attributes are not individual traits to be picked from, but they are to be seen as a whole: the description of a person who is redeemed and living for the Lord. There is no law against this sort of lifestyle. In fact, people with this level of devotion and these qualities tend to be recognized by the world as good, godly individuals. It is the Holy Spirit living in us and helping us that grows this fruit in our lives and helps us turn away from an otherwise sinful, deplorable existence.

What examples of the fruit of the Spirit do you see in your own life and in the life of your spouse?

Incomprehensible

Do you think lightly of the riches of His kindness and tolerance and patience, not knowing that the kindness of God leads you to repentance?
ROMANS 2:4 NASB

Not a single person is without sin. We do not live by a system that is based on our good works outnumbering our bad works because anyone who is imperfect cannot go before a perfect King. Every sin separates us from God, but he offers redemption through grace. We should not become complacent because of grace, but we should also not fool ourselves into believing that we are free from punishment because of the good things we do. Every sin is detestable. If we believe we are relatively good people deserving of forgiveness, we deceive ourselves and have not experienced the incomprehensible kindness of God that has offered us our only chance at redemption.

Through the blood of Christ, we repent of our sins, accepting the kindness of our King. His patience with us, and not our own virtues, is what is needed for salvation. We ought not judge the sins of others outside of the love of Christ. His love is available to all mankind, regardless of how we view them.

If not for salvation, what is the purpose of denying sinful lusts and living a righteous life?

Unafraid

I will not be afraid, because the LORD is with me.
People can't do anything to me.

PSALM 118:6 NCV

From time to time fear gets the best of us. It is an illness of the soul; it immobilizes us as it paralyzes our spirit and fills our flesh with dread. Fear can hijack our minds and drive us away from trusting God. It prompts us to rely on our own strength, forsaking the wisdom and power of the Almighty, which is why the Bible addresses it so frequently. When tragedy overtakes us or imposing threats wreak havoc on our hearts, it is easy to take our gaze off God and replace our faith with fear. This crippling mistake leaves our hearts in shambles. It also prevents us from living an effective Christian life and from reaching out to others with the good news of the Gospel.

God's Word assures us that he is always with us and we need not be fearful. We should be controlled by the Spirit of God and not a spirit of fear. Sometimes we even fear things that do not have eternal bearing instead of fearing God who is all powerful—the origin of all things everlasting. People and earthly threats can only harm us physically. Let us submit to the only one who holds our eternal lives in his loving hands.

Do you have any fears you need to lay before the Lord?

Replacing Ashes

I will give them a crown to replace their ashes,
and the oil of gladness to replace their sorrow,
and clothes of praise to replace their spirit of sadness.

ISAIAH 61:3 NCV

Although we live in a depraved world, God has given us a beautiful tool to help us along the way: his promises and the hope found therein. God has assured us that he will turn our tears into dancing, and our morning into shouts of joy! We can rest in the fact that whatever happens, no matter how dark our surroundings become, we have a future of goodness and light waiting for us.

Our Father intends to use us to display his glory, so we can be sure that he has wonderful plans for us. God loves us very deeply and desires only good things for us, but the sad truth is that in this world we will suffer sometimes before those good things are revealed. Do not despair if you are experiencing hardships, it does not mean God has forsaken you. Hold onto the truth that he will give you a new life and that the evil of this world will pass away.

Can you imagine a love so strong that it can replace
all your sorrow with joy in a single moment?

Rekindle the Flame

If I had the gift of prophecy, and if I understood all of God's secret plans and possessed all knowledge, and if I had such faith that I could move mountains, but didn't love others, I would be nothing. If I gave everything I have to the poor and even sacrificed my body, I could boast about it; but if I didn't love others, I would have gained nothing.

1 CORINTHIANS 13:1-3 NLT

Love trumps all! Every spiritual gift could be ours and we could possess the wisdom of Solomon and sacrifice all we have, but without love, it is meaningless. The building blocks of a good marriage are varied—among them trust, compatibility, common interests, attraction, and passion. However, if there is no love, the relationship cannot exist.

Love covers; love is selfless; love seeks the other's good, and puts the other first. Love allows discussions and decisions to happen in peace because there is an innate desire to please the other. Self-sacrifice comes easily and joyfully.

If you feel like the love factor has diminished
in your marriage, can you figure out why?
Sit down with your mate and discuss
how you can reclaim your first love.

Our Struggle

Our struggle is not against flesh and blood, but against the rulers,
against the powers, against the world forces of this darkness,
against the spiritual forces of wickedness in the heavenly places.

EPHESIANS 6:12 NASB

As we consider the condition of the world, it is easy to become fixated on the enemies we can see. Those who prey on the vulnerable, who exploit others for gain, who take pleasure in the suffering of others can seem like our most impending adversaries, but they are only puppets on the hands of the devil. Our actual enemy, the ruler of darkness, is the one who influences people to sin and who works them into his own evil ploys.

Before becoming too focused on the physical enemies we can see, we should consider the bigger picture and pray that God would open our eyes so we understand the actual battles we are confronted with. Then, in lieu of the verses before and after this accurate battle assessment, we should equip ourselves with the armor of God which is the only way to beat a demonic enemy: truth, righteousness, the Gospel of peace, faith, salvation, and the Word of God.

How can you and your spouse fight
spiritual forces of wickedness together?

Half Empty Cup

The Berean Jews were of more noble character than those in Thessalonica,
for they received the message with great eagerness and examined the
Scriptures every day to see if what Paul said was true.

ACTS 17:11 NIV

It is often said that opposites attract. In a marriage, the husband
and the wife each bring strengths and weaknesses to the relationship.
One spouse might have the propensity to see things in a negative
light, while the other has a more optimistic outlook. Different
people have different temperaments. The optimist can encourage the
pessimist to lighten up and see the fun in life. The pessimist needs to
grow in trust and gratitude to begin to see life through a new lens—
one focused on God's goodness and blessings.

What is your outlook? Are you the eternal optimist, always seeing
the good? Or are you a pessimist, desperately needing someone
to help you see that there is light at the end of the tunnel? A
great marriage is one where there is mutual encouragement and
willingness to grow and change.

Is your cup half full or half empty?
Do you look at the bright side of everything,
or do you need your mate to help you lighten up?
Talk about your differences.

Discipline Challenge

Discipline your children, and they will give you rest;
they will give delight to your heart.

PROVERBS 29:17 NRSV

Every parent knows that having children will entail many sleepless nights. These can be draining and discouraging, but it is a worthwhile and eternal investment in the kingdom of God. Children are a blessing, and they are also a formidable undertaking. By righteously disciplining our children even when we do not want to, it teaches them boundaries and healthy habits. By helping our children develop self-discipline, we instill in them godly character traits that will help them tremendously throughout life.

It brings such peace of mind to know that our children have a relationship with the Lord and have been raised in a way that they have a matured sense of right from wrong. In those days we can rest because we put the time in when they are young to love and discipline them in the ways of the Lord.

Do you have children in your life?
How can you and your spouse help create
healthy disciplines in their lives?

Planting Seeds

Start children off on the way they should go
and even when they are old they will not turn from it.
PROVERBS 22:6 NIV

Were you trained properly while you were growing up? Very few of us were. No matter. God can bless and train even the most flawed of humanity if they are convicted to repent. Any person, regardless of their upbringing, can give themselves fully to the Lord and live the life of purpose that God intends for them. That said, are you and your spouse now parents? Do you fully embrace the purpose in parenting that the Lord has laid out for us in the Bible? We have a beautiful and ponderous responsibility to introduce our children to the Creator of all and how we were raised does not factor into this responsibility.

We can depend upon God to teach and train us even for this task because the family is the heart of ministry. We have a responsibility to our children and to realize that their upbringing is for the purpose of leading them into the kingdom. Each life lesson, each math class, each good manner is taught with the purpose of edifying God and growing our children's hearts toward him. When we are united in our marriage to teach and train our children in the ways of God, we are fulfilling one of the most basic tasks of teaching others about Christ.

*Have you and your spouse committed
to introducing your children to the Lord?*

Always a Child

Children, obey your parents because you belong to the Lord, for this is
the right thing to do. "Honor your father and mother." This is the first
commandment with a promise: If you honor your father and mother,
"things will go well for you, and you will have a long life on the earth."

EPHESIANS 6:1-3 NLT

The relationship between a parent and child is another fitting
analogy of God's relationship with us. At times, we do not
understand why God asks us to do what he does. We do not always
like his rules and sometimes we wish we could wander off. Naturally,
we want to do things that make us feel good, like a child wishes to
eat only sweets. Like a good parent, God teaches us to have self-
discipline, make wise choices, follow his leadership even when we do
not have the full picture, and eat our vegetables.

In reference to the Ten Commandments, Paul notes that this is the
first of God's laws that is accompanied by a promise. Not only does
God bless obedience of both young and grown children when we
honor our parents by being respectful toward them, but it stands
to reason in the natural world that someone who has learned
obedience and humility toward authority will have a much easier
time in life than a defiant and egocentric person.

How can you honor your parents even today as an adult?
How can you respect them when you disagree with them?

Father of Comfort

Praise be to the God and Father of our Lord Jesus Christ,
the Father of compassion and the God of all comfort.

2 CORINTHIANS 1:3 NIV

Paul had recently gone through a distressing time of torture where
he was near death, so when he wrote this praise to the church in
Corinth that God is the Father of all comfort, he personally knew it
to be true. His faith had not wavered in the face of persecution even
though his body had. More than anything else in life, Paul knew
that God was with him offering him compassion, comfort, and an
everlasting hope.

Our ultimate Judge who rules with justice also extends mercy to
anyone who will receive it. He hears the cries of those who mourn
and is near to those who suffer. We all deserve his wrath, yet he
welcomes us with open arms. In this world of striving, suffering,
failing, and deception, we know that God is true. He is not absent
or uncaring but involved and accessible. We can run to him for rest,
peace, encouragement, acceptance, comfort, compassion, and truth.

What sort of help do you need to ask God for today?

Time Marches On

Do not forget this one thing, dear friends:
With the Lord a day is like a thousand years,
and a thousand years are like a day.

2 PETER 3:8 NIV

False teachers were claiming that Christ would not return and that there would be no Judgment Day. Their reasoning was that he had not yet returned, so why did he tarry? Peter's retort was that God is not bound by time and space. Our thinking is linear, in terms of minutes, hours, days, and years. God does not think like that since he is outside of time. His reasoning is dependable, and his plan is flawless.

Although it may seem like he is taking too long with all the injustice and evil that has plagued this world, God's timing is perfect. He knows the optimal moment for his return because he holds all of history and can see the heart of every person. None of us know the time when Christ will return, so we can only pray and continue in obedience. We should not judge his patience or forget his promises. Everything he has ever promised he will fulfill. We can have confidence that he will come back when the time is right.

How can you encourage your spouse
to be patient about God's timing?

The Waiting Game

"Love your enemies and pray
for those who persecute you."
MATTHEW 5:44 ESV

Injustice hurts most of us deeply. To see a neighbor, family member, or even a stranger being hurt is sometimes too much. We must remember that in the end, God is the judge, and he is just. Punishment will be rendered for evil deeds. We must be careful, though, to not hate our enemies. The Bible commands us to love them.

We should pray for redemption for sinners, that they would turn from their sin and be saved. Sometimes it is hard to pray for our enemies because we would rather see them hurt or punished, but that is not what God wants for us. To harbor such bitterness is poison for our hearts. Righteous anger is sometimes warranted, but we must keep perspective and remember that the Lord is with us. He fights for us, and we should neither be afraid nor vile in return. To remain kind to your enemies is only possible through praying and communion with the Lord.

Are you harboring anger against an enemy?

Control Factor

Whoever is slow to anger is better than the mighty,
and he who rules his spirit than he who takes a city.
PROVERBS 16:32 ESV

The desire to control has been an issue since the beginning of time. Wars have been fought; divorces have occurred; deaths have resulted from people vying for control. Marriage was created by God, not as a competition, but as a partnership. The battle to control has no place in marriage other than each partner developing self-control. Decisions, satisfactory to both, should be made by discussion, mutual agreement, and prayer.

God is our ultimate authority, and he is in charge. A good marriage operates from the framework where neither is struggling to control. Both are working together to accomplish the responsibilities set before them in an amicable fashion. The marriage benefits as the work is divided and decisions mutually made, always acknowledging God as the director. Be patient with each other and enjoy peace.

Are there issues in your marriage where you struggle
for control? How best could you rectify those?

Personality Clashes

If possible, so far as it depends on you,
live peaceably with all.
ROMANS 12:18 ESV

People are unique individuals with distinct personalities. Occasionally you may meet someone who is difficult to get along with and you soon realize that your personalities don't automatically jive. It may take some work to develop and maintain such a relationship. You may find that to be true in your marriage. Initially, you were attracted to your mate perhaps because of his or her good looks. Maybe you discovered a talent or trait that was especially endearing. You learned you had common interests and shared similar values.

Even after all you knew, you undoubtedly discovered some new things after marriage—habits, personality quirks, and different ways of seeing things that cause occasional disagreements. What happened to the peace and joy you once experienced, and, more importantly, what is to be done? According to Scripture, look within. Ask God to reveal to you the ways you are contributing to the discord and open your eyes to your own difficult personality traits. Such a prayer will open the door for God to begin a transformation in your heart that will affect you both.

What are some of the personality differences between you and your mate? Ask God to reveal where each of you needs to change and to grant the grace to accept one another.

Getting Along

Make every effort to live in peace with everyone and to be holy;
without holiness no one will see the Lord.

HEBREWS 12:14 NIV

Marriage not only brings times of sweetness and flowers, but also times of disagreement and even strife. Once you are united in marriage and living under one roof, you soon discover that the two of you do not see eye to eye on everything. Decisions lie ahead, and your spouse's view may go against your grain and aggravate your sense of logic. Are you going to argue, each insisting on your own way, or are you going to compromise for the sake of peace? At times, even silence is wise as you both take the time to process your thoughts and ask God for guidance.

The goal is to have a peaceful home. Peace fosters growth both in your relationship to God and to each other. When new patterns of conflict resolution become a habit, disagreements won't be as frequent and peace will reign. The New Living Translation puts it this way: "Work at living in peace with everyone, and work at living a holy life, for those who are not holy will not see the Lord."

Does God's peace rule in your home?
If not, what can you do differently?

Smart People

Those with good sense are slow to anger,
and it is their glory to overlook an offense.

PROVERBS 19:11 NRSV

*I*t is only through wisdom that we can establish inner calmness. By slowing our anger and holding our tongues we can learn far more than otherwise. Wisdom and patience go hand in hand, just as philosophy and virtue always should. In our current world, the unangered, unperturbed person is rarely heralded as a source of truth. We look to loud showboats instead of role models of patience. The second half of the verse is equally countercultural. What person became famous in our world because they overlooked an offense?

All too often we are inspired by what makes us feel good; doing to others what they have done to us. Yet the unsatisfying option of forgiveness is often thrown out the window. For this reason, God assigns it to be our glory to overlook transgressions. The moment we forgo our natural instincts and render supernatural forgiveness to an enemy, we become a little more like Jesus Christ. He alone had the power to overlook every transgression, and through him we can display forgiveness as well.

*How can you drown out the noise of those screaming in anger
and hear the melodical, timeless voice of truth?*

Faithful in Prayer

Be joyful in hope, patient in affliction, faithful in prayer.

ROMANS 12:12 NIV

*O*ne of the most valuable gifts we have in our marriages is prayer. When we learn to trust in God and turn our problems over to him, there's an inexplicable joy and a sweet hope that comes, even when the circumstances haven't changed. Times of affliction are tough, especially when our spouse is affected. Our first inclination is to try to fix the problem and so often we can't. How wonderful to know the God who can! Continue to pray, even when you don't see the answer in front of you. And while you are waiting, ask the Lord what he wants you to learn from the situation.

There's a special sweetness that comes when couples pray together. A wonderful heritage is being crafted prayer by prayer, and one day will be looked back on with gratitude at the faithfulness of God. Hearts are bonded side by side.

Do you pray together as a couple? Take a moment to remember the answers to prayer you have received.

Beyond the List

"Call to me and I will answer you and tell you
great and unsearchable things you do not know."
JEREMIAH 33:3 NIV

God tells us to call out to him and he will answer. This
unchanging offer is one of the kindest acts of love our Savior offers.
He does not just consider answering us, he promised he will.
Considering our infinite lowliness, Christ's ineffable glory, and
the chasm between us, there is no reason that our Creator would
be obligated to give us his attention; yet he does. Further still, he
promises that those who come to him will learn great things which
cannot be learned elsewhere.

When people of other religions open their sacred books, they only
learn what humankind can do in and of themselves. The writings
are only the thoughts of people. Yet here God points us to himself,
saying that he can tell us unsearchable things that we don't know.
Only a real God can know things outside the human realm of
knowledge. There are many of these unsearchable things which God
would reveal to us should we take the time to seek his Word and call
to him.

*What great and mighty mysteries has God revealed to you
when you sought him?*

No Fear

She laughs without fear of the future.
PROVERBS 31:25 NLT

How much does your faith dictate your behavior? Have you committed yourself daily to saturating your heart in the Word, allowing the Holy Spirit to craft and curb your personality? Can you say that this is more important to you than the way you look? Can you say that your faith is such that the future looks joyful, that you have no fear that cannot be overcome by your love for God?

So much of our path through life is mediated by our perceptions and personalities. We can hedge against the distractions that take us away from God's chosen trail by fully allowing the Scriptures to sink into our hearts and soften our manner. We can know that God is near all the time by spending time in his presence daily, hourly, with every breath. Keep your conversation with the Lord going. Talk to him as you walk along your path, giving him the voice in your life that he desires and you need. Let your love for him overcome all the interruptions so you are joyful and strong in your faith and your marriage.

Is your dependence on God clearly seen
in your strength and dignity?
Do you rest on your faith in God
instead of plans and resources?

Hearts Aligned

This is the confidence we have in approaching God:
that if we ask anything according to his will, he hears us.

1 JOHN 5:14 NIV

Have you ever tried to communicate with your spouse while their mind was elsewhere, and your words were unheard? Perhaps you asked your mate to pick up some coffee filters and creamer on the way home, but since no mental notes were made in the first place, it was forgotten. Or maybe there's something you want to ask, but you're nervous and afraid the request will cause conflict or won't be taken in the right way.

In contrast, you never have to worry about any of that when you come to God. You can be confident that whenever you approach him, he hears every word you say—even to the extent of knowing the unspoken requests that are too difficult for you to verbalize. Husbands and wives, do you have a request today? Ask in accordance with his will, and rest secure in the knowledge that you have been heard.

Is prayer a big part of your marriage?
Are you confident that when you bring your needs to God,
he really does hear you?

Chase After God

Seek the LORD while you can find him. Call on him now while he is near.
Let the wicked change their ways and banish the very thought of doing
wrong. Let them turn to the LORD that he may have mercy on them.
Yes, turn to our God, for he will forgive generously.

ISAIAH 55:6-7 NLT

There are times in everyone's life when God's presence is especially close. Under the pressure of great pain and trouble, even an unbeliever's heart can become more open to the Lord's voice. This is what Isaiah wants us to notice. He wants us to lay hold of Christ when pain makes God especially near to us. The question is, will we? Will we cry out to God when he knocks on our door; will we turn to him when the pain becomes too much to bear? Otherwise, we might dismiss God. We could consider him an irrational notion, unmerciful, or unable to understand us.

These are the doubts that withhold sinners from eternal peace. Turning to God is not only meant for the righteous or noble, but also the unrighteous sinner. Even they will find compassion from God should they call to him. Anyone who seeks the Lord will be abundantly pardoned. There is no condition. God knows that we have nothing to offer, so he draws near to us and pleads that we seek him while he may be found.

*In the midst of trials, what other things distract you
from seeking God for mercy?*

Run First

Look to the LORD and his strength;
seek his face always.
1 CHRONICLES 16:11 NIV

In everyday problems, the Lord's strength is an unusual source of help. It may seem too esoteric to rely on, yet the Word of God commands us to seek God and his strength because it is real and effective. Even before our own attempts fail, we should look to God and his ability to accomplish all things. Through this we come to see how small our problems, achievements, goals, and failures really are.

There is no better cure for anxiety than the sight of God's infinite strength and favor. What are we struggling to do on our own? Just as we look for food in order to survive, our spirit continually needs the Lord in order to thrive. No one can do anything without seeking God's help. We may skip a time of devotion without feeling worse, like when we skip lunch, but in both cases it is the cumulative impact that wreaks havoc. The author of this verse commands us to seek God's face continually because it will make our spirits live. Anxiety, doubt, greed, and every other disease of the soul is cured by seeking him.

*What happens when you do not seek the Lord
for strength in a situation?*

The Priority

Without faith it is impossible to please God, because anyone who comes to him must believe that he exists and that he rewards those who earnestly seek him.

HEBREWS 11:6 NIV

We were not designed to be submissive servants of a god who is only interested in obedience. He carefully crafted us to display his glorious nature. He intended us to be his friends because he loves fellowship. We were given free will because God wants to be chosen; he wants our worship to be given from an adoring heart not demanded of a slave in subjection to their master.

The Lord does require obedience, but the priority is our faith. From faith will come obedience because our hearts long to serve and please him. He gave us life, and we joyfully surrender our lives back to him. He does not need to demand compliance from those who have truly experienced his love because we earnestly seek him. Without faith, it does not matter how much good we do. God is not satisfied with the deeds of those who simply go through the religious motions; what he longs for is a loving relationship.

Do you find it easier to serve your spouse because you know it will bring them joy than when you are just trying to uphold your marital duties for the sake of expectation?

Lens of Love

There is one body and one Spirit, just as you were called to one hope when you were called; one Lord, one faith, one baptism; one God and Father of all, who is over all and through all and in all.

EPHESIANS 4:4-6 NIV

The church of Christ is not a building or a select group of Christians but a body of believers which includes everyone who has given their life and allegiance to Jesus Christ. Although there may be differences of opinion regarding theology or practice, the fundamental truths remain the same. God is one and we have the hope of eternity through Christ. Because we are one body of believers serving the same God, we share the same faith. We cannot allow variance to divide us and distract us from our mandate to love each other.

In the end, it is God who judges the hearts of men and women not us. As we navigate our differences and learn from each other, we should view our brothers and sisters in Christ through a lens of love, since that is how God views us. This does not mean denying differences or falsifying feelings but recognizing that differences are an opportunity for growth.

How do you approach conversations where you have a differing opinion than your spouse?

New Mercies

The steadfast love of the LORD never ceases;
his mercies never come to an end;
they are new every morning;
great is your faithfulness.

LAMENTATIONS 3:22-23 ESV

Every morning is a fresh start and a new opportunity to love.
We have been given the blessed privilege of marriage and we have
the distinct responsibility of demonstrating Christ-like love to our
spouses every single day. Love is not a one-time gift or agreement;
it is constantly refreshed and given over and over. Just as God never
ceases to pursue us and draw us to himself, we ought to continue
looking for new ways to demonstrate our love to our spouses. The
faithfulness of God sets a precedence for our own conduct. He has
always remained true to his promises. We are his beloved bride, and
he declares his adoration of us.

Similarly, we should be resolute in our commitment to our spouses.
With undivided love and adherence to our vows, we uphold
marriage as a symbol of the love we have been given. When we
make mistakes, God is merciful and willing to help us stand back up.
When we stumble, he catches us. Although we are weak, he fills us
with strength and courage to maintain our resolve to follow him and
stay loyal to our spouses.

*Does the Lord's faithfulness to you give you the resolve
to be faithful to your spouse?*

Deep Yearnings

> "For this child I prayed, and the LORD has granted me my petition
> which I asked of Him. Therefore I also have lent him to the LORD;
> as long as he lives he shall be lent to the LORD."
>
> 1 SAMUEL 1:27-28 NKJV

Hannah grieved deeply because she had no children. Her husband's other wife added to her misery by rubbing it in her face that she was barren. In brokenness and despair, she went before the Lord and asked for a child. The Lord had mercy on her and granted her a son! When the child, Samuel, was old enough, she dedicated him to the Lord for fulltime ministry. Each of our stories is going to be different, but the lessons learned from Hannah's gratefulness and God's grace can be applied to any of us.

Our Father does not owe us anything, yet he chooses to give good gifts. In reverent thankfulness we need to remember it was him who gave us the good gifts and see how we can use them for his service and praise. Our marriages could be one example of this. God has given us an amazing blessing in the form of our spouse! How can we dedicate our marriages to the Lord as a form of praise and demonstration of gratefulness?

What has God given you that you can use to serve him?

April

Love is large and incredibly patient.
Love is gentle and consistently kind to all.
It refuses to be jealous when blessing comes
to someone else. Love does not brag about one's
achievements nor inflate its own importance.

1 CORINTHIANS 13:4 TPT

Way of Fools

The way of fools seems right to them,
but the wise listen to advice.

PROVERBS 12:15 NIV

It is natural for us to believe we are right, and others are wrong when it comes to matters of dispute. A fool will not heed correction nor consider other perspectives. A wise person recognizes that everyone has room to grow and learn. None of us hold all the answers, and all of us have been wrong at times. Therefore, rather than disregarding a person or an idea before you have humbly reflected on the matter, pray and ask God to reveal his truth. Listen to wise counsel and advice. Learn to put biased and preconceived notions to the side and be teachable.

Wise people know they do not have to prove their worth or defend themselves because God has already accepted them, and he is their defender. Consider the words of your spouse especially because God gave us marriage as a gift. Refuse to be foolish and listen to what your beloved gift from God is saying. Two minds and hearts working as one can accomplish and understand far more than either one can individually.

Are you open to hearing advice?
How do you react to being wrong?

Ask the Teacher

If any of you lacks wisdom, you should ask God,
who gives generously to all without finding fault,
and it will be given to you.

JAMES 1:5 NIV

The Scriptures explain often how we can acquire wisdom. In this instance, James is referring to specific situations. When we are confronted with a decision and we do not know how to proceed, we ask God for wisdom to know what to do in that moment. Making the decision to not haphazardly run forward but taking the time to inquire of God instead protects us from foolhardy choices and regrettable outcomes.

When we seek God, the Bible says he gives wisdom generously. He is not stingy, nor is he hidden. He is nearby and willing. The greatest source of wisdom is God himself, although he has also established other avenues we can receive wisdom from. He has given us his Word, and he encourages us to seek advice from wise counselors.

Is there anything you need wisdom for today?

Billions of Cells

You created my inmost being; you knit me together in my mother's womb.
I praise you because I am fearfully and wonderfully made;
your works are wonderful, I know that full well.

PSALM 139:13-14 NIV

Human life is a marvelous thing. The Almighty so intrinsically crafted each person exactly how he intended them to be. Every person has a unique design, a calling, and God's fingerprint on them. He created us in his image, and yet his being is so vast and so wonderful none of us could carry it all! So, each of us displays a piece of our heavenly Father.

We should remember this when we consider the unborn. Although we cannot see or hear them, their Maker can, and he cares for them. We should also remember this when we consider our enemies. Perhaps there are powerful people who oppress us and what we stand for, or perhaps we have personal squabbles with others who wish us harm. Whatever the case, every person has been fearfully and wonderfully made by God, and he loves them dearly.

What do you find amazing
about the way your spouse was created?

Stressful Marathons

We have this treasure in jars of clay to show that this all-surpassing power is from God and not from us. We are hard pressed on every side, but not crushed; perplexed, but not in despair; persecuted, but not abandoned; struck down, but not destroyed.

2 CORINTHIANS 4:7-9 NIV

We are similar in structure to jars made from clay. God created us to carry his light and love to the world. By opening our hearts and lives to his leading, he fills us with his power which cannot be overcome. There are many evils things at work in this world, but our Lord of Light is more powerful than they are.

Although there will be times when we feel like the weight of the world is too much for a simple earthen pot, the authority of Jehovah, which he has placed in us, can withstand it. Despite the perplexing problems we face, we need never despair because he has given us an everlasting hope. Even if we face persecution, he will never abandon us. All this world can do is strike us down or even kill us, but it cannot destroy us because it is God who saves and preserves us. Our home is with him.

When you feel like the pressures of life are too great for you to handle, what can you do to persevere in a godly manner?

Shield of Love

You bless the godly, O LORD;
you surround them with your shield of love.

PSALM 5:12 NIV

We can have confidence in the Lord's judgment. He blesses the godly, punishes the wicked, and avenges the oppressed. Like a giant shield is the Lord's protection. The shield David uses as a comparison in this verse is a standing shield which covered the entire body of a warrior. Our caring Father shields us all around from every attack of the enemy, and he does so with his love.

No matter what happens to our mortal bodies, the Lord's love will sustain us because he has saved us from death's grip before we even face that ultimate enemy. Just like the grave could not hold the Lord Jesus, it cannot hold those who belong to him. He has blessed the godly with his divine protection, his eternal love, and life everlasting.

How does knowing the Lord's love surrounds you
as a protective shield change the way you
approach difficulties in your life?

Just Stay Calm

The LORD himself will fight for you.
Just stay calm.

EXODUS 14:14 NLT

Anyone can talk a big game, but when circumstances are truly bad and it becomes obvious that we do not have control over the outcomes that affect us, our responses betray where our confidence lies. If we are relying on our own strength to carry us through life's obstacles, then when we inevitably become ensnared, our reaction will be desperate and unwise.

Yet, if our lives are hidden in Christ, and we have learned to look to him for our power, then regardless of the circumstances that threaten to take us down, we know that the Lord will intervene on our behalf. He fights our battles, so we need only to trust in him and remain calm. Real life circumstances will reveal whether we are vainly striving for self-sufficiency or wisely placing our trust in the Lord.

How do you react when life gets out of control?

Safe and Secure

God, hear my cry; listen to my prayer.
I call to you from the ends of the earth when I am afraid.
Carry me away to a high mountain.
You have been my protection,
like a strong tower against my enemies.

PSALM 61:1 NCV

Have you ever visited a Medieval castle? These fortresses were built in such a way that they could protect entire villages against an enemy's attack. There were food storage rooms and a water supply in case the siege lasted a long time. There were towers and high walls for protection and battle. The Lord is your castle. He can protect you from fear and worry. He will supply all your needs. Just as the villagers could run to the castle and be safe within its walls, God will draw you near to him and wrap his arms around you.

No matter the circumstances, whatever you face, God can and will protect and defend you in times of difficulty. Relax, rest in him, feel secure in his ability to help. Remember he is your shield and your protector in times of need. Let him fight your battles.

What is your response to fear and anxiety?
When you face worrisome problems do you ask for God's help?
Can you remember a time when you
felt safely supported by him?

Stepping Away

Your mercy reaches unto the heavens,
and your truth unto the clouds.

PSALM 57:10 NKJV

The entire universe is too small to contain God's love. So extravagant is it that he gave his very life to save us. Trying to comprehend that the King of the universe knelt in the dust and washed his friends' feet is absurd! Yet he did. He subjected himself to every vile element of life as a human because his love was that great. The disciples could see how much he cared for them, and that taught them to care for others in his name. God's love spreads like wildfire and has power to conquer every enemy. Even death itself could not thwart God's plan. His faithfulness is evident in everything around us.

All God's promises have already been or will be fulfilled, and he never forsakes his children. The heavens declare God's mercy, for the sun, moon, and stars offer life and balance and beauty. They stretch across the sky, observable and constant, reminding us of the wonders God created. It is through the mercy Christ showed us and the truth of the message he came to share that his love bridged the gap between heaven and earth.

How does the rainbow remind us of God's covenant with Noah?
How do the stars remind us of God's covenant with Abraham?
Why do you think he created the heavens and all its wonders?

Clothed in Righteousness

Let us behave decently, as in the daytime,
not in carousing and drunkenness,
not in sexual immorality and debauchery,
not in dissension and jealousy.

ROMANS 13:13 NIV

Sin hates the light because it reveals what it wants to hide. The nighttime is known for immoral acts because there are less eyes watching and darkness covers the deeds. During the day, people put on their best façade and present themselves as they want the world to see them. God always sees us, however, and he is the one whose opinion matters the most. It is his heart we hurt when we chose to act immorally.

As Christians devoted to purity of heart, not just appearance, how we act in secret should be just as honest as how we act in the streets during broad daylight. Carousing and drunkenness are aspects of a reckless, irresponsible individual. Sexual immorality and debauchery stem from someone who is seeking their own personal pleasure above God's standards. Dissension and jealousy happen when we care about our own gain instead of submitting to one another in love. Let us turn from indecent living and choose instead to be clothed in righteousness. The Lord's way is always the best way and will never lead to disappointment.

Is there anything you have kept hidden that you need to repent of and ask for God's help to turn away from?

Godly Contentment

There is great gain in godliness with contentment,
for we brought nothing into the world,
and we cannot take anything out of the world.
But if we have food and clothing, with these we will be content.

1 TIMOTHY 6:6-8 ESV

Contentment is a key feature of a person who is living for God and not for themselves. We came into this world with nothing and we will leave it with nothing as well. To spend our days chasing wealth is a waste of life that could be devoted to something meaningful and eternal. The Bible does not speak against having wealth only against allowing it to become your master and pursuit.

Whether we have great riches or are poverty-stricken, we are to be content with what God has blessed us with. The great gain this verse refers to is everything that is rewarded with living a godly and content life: joy, peace, satisfaction, and a spiritual life which is equipped to overcome the world's temptations and snares. Constantly chasing luxuries and material possessions will only rob us of the rich life we can experience when we are content with the gifts we have been given.

What has God given to you and your spouse
that you are thankful for today?

Triumphant Wisdom

The fear of the LORD is the beginning of knowledge,
But fools despise wisdom and instruction.

PROVERBS 1:7 NKJV

God created us as life-long learners; he wants us to gain wisdom. Wisdom comes liberally to those who ask for it. Sometimes, it comes from the School of Hard Knocks. Godly wisdom comes not only from the Bible, but also from those who study, teach, and preach it.

We are wise to watch and learn from the follies and successes of others. Positioning yourself among experienced people is not an act of weakness; it's a triumph of wisdom. It's common for a child to watch an older sibling's tactics, for good or bad. Did they get away with it, or was there trouble? Did they keep practicing and win the trophy?

Are you willing to find people who are smarter, kinder,
gentler, or wiser than yourself and learn from them?
Are you able to ask for advice?
Talk together about the people who are
good influences on your lives and marriage.

Gentle Answer

A gentle answer will calm a person's anger,
but an unkind answer will cause more anger.

PROVERBS 15:1 NCV

It is one thing to be right, and another thing to create change. By insensitively asserting ourselves, even if we are justified in what we are saying, we may lose more than we gain by intensifying the anger of the other person. If we truly care to create peace and calm the situation, gentleness can diffuse a situation and still get the point across. We do not have to shirk away from sharing what is true, but we do need to be kind.

Daniel and his friends could have outright refused to eat the forbidden meat of the king, stood their ground, and been persecuted for their godly convictions. They would not have influenced anyone positively, however. Instead, they chose to respectfully request that the king test their theory that they would actually be able to serve him better if they ate the way their God had instructed them to. God's way really was better, as evidenced through the young men, and the king's heart was moved. Simply by using a gentle approach, they changed the course of history and ultimately influenced an entire kingdom.

When you and your spouse get into a disagreement,
how can you talk it through without anger taking over?

Standards of Love

"Do not judge,
or you too will be judged."
MATTHEW 7:1 NIV

Following this verse are instructions on how to judge others properly, so this is not a command to never judge. Jesus warns his disciples to judge righteously, not based on outward appearances, so evidently there is a proper way to judge. As Christians, we are called to judge the difference between truth and untruth and to hold each other accountable. What Jesus is referring to in this command is to not judge the motivations of someone else's heart because only God knows what is there. We are not God, and we do not get to bestow condemnation on anyone.

One of the spiritual issues of that time were pompous practices of piety and good deeds on display. There was such an emphasis on righteous living that people were purposefully making big scenes and gestures so others would notice their virtue. They would also judge the actions and intents of those who perhaps did not showcase their generosity to the same degree. God hates hypocrisy. We need to act out of love and respect for God.

Do you question the motives of others, including your spouse?
How can you practice good judgment?

A Good Argument

Remind everyone about these things,
and command them in God's presence to stop fighting over words.
Such arguments are useless, and they can ruin those who hear them.

2 TIMOTHY 2:14 NLT

A bad apple can spoil the whole bushel. A bad word spoils a conversation. We know a soft answer turns away anger, but sometimes bruising words tumble out. We may just want to be heard, to know that what we say has worth. Sometimes we act out of conviction, wanting the other person to know that our way is the correct way of doing something.

It is a privilege to listen to each other and affirm your right to each think as you please. It is a hard right to submit to, especially when we know the person has set a destructive course. Sometimes, a person just enjoys a good argument. A spouse might want to complain to the other without hearing a solution. Keep each other's preferences in mind when tensions rise.

Do you enjoy a good argument?
Do you try to fix a complaint when your
hurting spouse just wants a sounding board?
Discuss what each of you needs in your communication with
each other especially when you might disagree on something.

Testing Patience

God is not man, that he should lie, or a son of man,
that he should change his mind. Has he said, and will he not do it?
Or has he spoken, and will he not fulfill it?

NUMBERS 23:19 ESV

We have all faced disappointment at one time or another by someone we knew and trusted. We have also likely been the cause of disappointment for someone else. We make promises that we cannot always keep. Sometimes we simply fail to keep them because of our own selfishness or oversight. This vice does not apply to our Father since he is perfect, and he has upheld every single one of his promises since the beginning of time.

Nothing that God has proclaimed in his Word is a lie or a mistake. He has never spoken an offhand remark that he later regretted. His words are dependable and they offer hope. Even when we fail to be faithful to God, he remains faithful to us because of his perfect character and his unmatched love. He will continue to fulfill every promise he has ever made, and we will see the whole story unfold exactly the way he intends it to.

How do you approach lying in your household?

Two Paths

Who is wise and understanding among you?
By his good conduct let him show his works in the meekness of wisdom.
JAMES 3:13 ESV

James asked a thought-provoking question about who has both understanding and wisdom. The Greek term for understanding is epistēmon, referring to the intellectual knowledge we attain. The word he used for wisdom is sophos which is our moral awareness and insight. Both are important, but James highlighted the use of wisdom through meekness as that which a true follower of Christ ought to be practicing.

Understanding can be attained, but wisdom is a gift reserved for those who walk with Lord and heed his voice. Those who have been given the gift of wisdom will be recognized through their good works done in meekness. Doing good deeds is not necessary for the attainment of either wisdom or salvation, but they are the result of a wise person who has been born again. It is admirable and beneficial to study the Word of God, to learn of his ways, to consider history, and to grow in our understanding. Yet greater still is to listen to the whispers of our Father, to meditate on his Word, to spend time walking with him, and to grow in meekness.

Why does wisdom change a person's conduct?
How does it change?

Judgment

"Do not judge others, and you will not be judged.
Do not condemn others, or it will all come back against you.
Forgive others, and you will be forgiven."

LUKE 6:37 NLT

Judgment in itself is not bad. We make judgments every day. Is the stove hot? Is it safe to cross the street? Biblical Abigail said that her husband, Nabal, was a foolish man, and the Bible tells us she had "good judgment." God does not require us to lie and say something is what it is not. What is this verse really talking about?

To cast judgment on someone is to revile them, and no good comes from it. Think of a ball thrown against a wall. The velocity of its return will be greater than when it was initially thrown. So too are the consequences of judging. To forgive someone does not mean they are not responsible for their actions or that you condone their behavior. Forgiveness brings freedom to both parties.

Are you bound by a grudge?
Have you been casting judgment on someone you need to free?
What can you do right now to begin the process of forgiveness?

Children of God

> To all who did accept him and believe in him
> he gave the right to become children of God.
>
> JOHN 1:12 NCV

Being part of a family gives us certain privileges. Even amid disagreements, there is a bond that unites family members that runs deeper than other relationships. Those of us who have been welcomed into God's family also experience rights and benefits that those who have estranged themselves to God are not privy to. As children of God, we have an eternal inheritance through Jesus Christ. We did not earn this inheritance, but our God is a loving Father who joyfully gives all good things to his children.

God's love is given, never earned, but being his child also comes with responsibilities. Since we are members of his family, we bear his name. This honor should cause us to realize just who it is we represent as we go about our days. Faith in Jesus Christ is an active, living faith that does not take for granted the price that was paid for our freedom from sin. Our lives should reflect the place we have in God's family and the freedom we have experienced through Christ's love and sacrifice.

What sort of privileges do children receive
from their earthly families?
What sort of privileges do we receive
from our eternal family under God?

Rewards

"I the LORD search the heart and examine the mind, to reward each person according to their conduct, according to what their deeds deserve."

JEREMIAH 17:10 NIV

People cannot read minds, which makes it easy to control the way we portray ourselves. God, however, is omniscient. He knows everything. The most fleeting thought that has passed through our minds, our strongest desires, our greatest weaknesses—he knows it all. God knows when we're doing something for selfish reasons, and when we are sincerely motivated. The Bible says that God searched us, and he knew all our days before they existed.

The good thing is that God is also incredibly loving and forgiving. Above anyone else, he is the safest place to share our hearts and to be open and honest. God does not expect perfection from us, all he wants is for us to give ourselves to him and his plan, trusting him in the process. When we work on keeping our thoughts pure and disciplining the way we think, God rewards us.

Does the idea of God knowing your thoughts make you uncomfortable?

Meeting Together

Let us not neglect our meeting together, as some people do,
but encourage one another,
especially now that the day of his return is drawing near.

HEBREWS 10:25 NLT

The emphasis on individualism and self-sufficiency is strong, but stronger still is the command to meet and encourage one another. As believers, we have been tasked with caring for each other as if we were all one body. This may not be a mandate which garners much attention, but we cannot overlook it. We were created for community and we need others around us to speak into our lives: to offer encouragement and insight.

Just like a predator attempts to draw its prey away from the herd, our enemy tries to isolate us and lead us astray. Together we are more powerful because we can help each other. This verse makes it clear that this commandment becomes ever more pertinent as time goes by. Every day, the end draws nearer, and this world becomes more and more uncertain. Now, more than ever before, we must not neglect our brothers and sisters in the Lord. Prioritize meeting together, sharing in each other's needs and burdens. Pray, cry, laugh, love, sing, eat, and be real together.

Who do you and your spouse meet with?
How can you encourage each other?

All Is Possible

"All things are possible
to him who believes."

MARK 9:23 NASB

Understanding the context of Jesus' words is necessary for deriving his intent. He is not saying that through belief in God we can do anything we want, but that belief in God means we know that he can do whatever he wants through us. All things are possible, and Jesus is the purpose. The disciples had been unsuccessful in casting a demon out of a little boy. The scribes did not believe that Jesus' powers were that of God's, and the father of the demon-possessed boy struggled with unbelief.

Jesus did not demand that the father feign belief, only that he be honest about where he was at and willing to receive. He begged Jesus to help him overcome his unbelief and Jesus did just that. He commanded the demon out of the boy and in doing so he saved the child, restored the father's faith, proved his deity to the skeptical scribes, taught the disciples to trust in the power of God, and demonstrated his healing power to the quickly gathering crowds! God can do all things; we only need to believe.

What challenge are you facing right now?
Do you believe God has the power to help you through it?
If you are doubting, have you asked your patient,
loving God to help you overcome your disbelief?

Vow to God

Sacrifice thank offerings to God,
fulfill your vows to the Most High,
and call on me in the day of trouble;
I will deliver you, and you will honor me.

PSALM 50:14-15 NIV

God does not take delight in worthless sacrifices from people while there is wickedness in their hearts. It is not our actions, sacrifices, or completion of religious duties that God desires, but an outpouring of our hearts in love for him. While it is good and blessed to do works of service for our Creator, the motive behind the motions should be birthed from a desire to please God and demonstrate our gratitude and loyalty. If our motive is to somehow vindicate ourselves or attempt to appear righteous, our offerings will not be accepted by God.

It is the Lord alone who vindicates us and makes us righteous, not what we do. The sacrifices that are acceptable before him come from a pure and upright heart that puts him above every other thing. The prophet Samuel once explained to King Saul that obedience is better than sacrifice. It is better to heed God's voice than to fulfill empty religious platitudes. He is moved by a pure heart and an upright mind.

What would you like to thank God for?
How can you and your spouse honor him today
in what you do and say?

Complementary Couple

The rib that the LORD God had taken from the man
he made into a woman and brought her to the man.
Then the man said, "This at last is bone of my bones and flesh of my flesh;
she shall be called woman because she was taken out of man."

GENESIS 2:22-23 ESV

When Yahweh created Adam, the process was defined by the Hebrew word *yiṣer* which implies shaping or molding something into existence. From Adam's own rib he formed Eve, and the term used for her creation was *banah* which means to add to something or to build it up even better. Yahweh made the two of them to complement each other and to be better together. As a couple, they were better than they were alone.

Although they were created differently, and we can observe that men and women are intrinsically different, both Adam and Eve were formed for the same purpose: to worship God and to be a blessing to each other. This union between a man and a woman was established before sin entered the world which teaches us that marriage was always part of God's perfect plan.

How do you and your spouse complement,
serve, and build each other up?
How are you different from each other?

Cherished Wisdom

The one who gets wisdom loves life.
The one who cherishes understanding will soon prosper.

PROVERBS 19:8 NIV

Life is already hard, but it is even harder for those who are unwise. They have no moral compass to guide them, and no timeless truth to catch them. The condition of our world underscores the value of wisdom in our daily lives. The kind of wisdom necessary for navigating this world is that which comes only from the Lord. The complexities of life daily confront us as we face a myriad of circumstances and choices that need to be addressed. Sometimes we make terrible choices or go down the wrong path when we fail to turn to the Lord for wisdom.

Obtaining wisdom greatly improves the choices we make and how we handle matters. Further, good choices naturally lead to a more fulfilled and prosperous life that extends beyond us and impacts those around us. Our spouses, other family members, friends, neighbors, and even strangers will all experience blessings because of the wise choices we make. The value of godly wisdom cannot be underestimated.

What sort of blessings have you received
because of the wisdom of your spouse?

Passing Through

We fix our eyes not on what is seen, but on what is unseen,
since what is seen is temporary, but what is unseen is eternal.

2 CORINTHIANS 4:18 NIV

*P*aul was enduring unimaginable suffering because of his faith;
so incredible was it that he admitted it was almost unbearable.
Still, in the face of his hardships, the words he wrote put back into
perspective the realness of eternity. In faith he declared that the
unseen promises of God were more real to him than the daily pain
and suffering he was enduring. His body was in turmoil, but his
hope was untouched. His gaze was set on the cross of Christ rather
than the temporary torture he was undergoing.

Transient trials cannot distract us from the heavenly hope hidden
in our hearts. We must fix our eyes on Jesus, for he is outside of
time. Briefer still than this world and its histories, are we, its human
inhabitants. Our lives last for a fleeting moment in time, but God
is outside of time and his reign is eternal. He has made a way for us
to live forever with him in his home, and this assurance is what has
captivated our hearts, minds, and attention. The world may have
its way for a while, but it will one day pass away and only what is
preserved with God will remain.

*How can you maintain an eternal perspective
while existing in a mortal, decaying world?*

Focus Forward

> One thing I do: Forgetting what is behind and straining toward what is ahead, I press on toward the goal to win the prize for which God has called me heavenward in Christ Jesus.
>
> PHILIPPIANS 3:13-14 NIV

None of us are where we would like to be morally. We all have room to grow, but maturity and sanctification is a process. Paul admitted that he had not fully grasped the depth of the impact Christ's resurrection had, but he continued in his spiritual walk which he likened to a race. To win a race, we must be committed to training and straining. It will stretch us and, at times, leave us exhausted, but the prize is worth it, so we continue to push forward.

In a race, turning to look back can be detrimental. Fixating on our past mistakes or comparing ourselves with other racers only slows us down and draws our attention away from the prize. Paul had many horrendous mistakes in his past, but he understood and accepted that Christ had removed the guilt of those from his record. His only objective now was to race after Christ at any cost. Having many goals will steal us away from focusing on the finish line. In life, it is not enough that Christ is our first goal, he ought to be our only goal and all other ambitions fall under submission to him.

How does having a spouse to race with you encourage you to press forward and not become distracted or fixated on the past?

Bringing Calm

Fools give full vent to their rage,
but the wise bring calm in the end.
PROVERBS 29:11 NIV

Have you ever gotten mad at your spouse, said ugly things, and then later wished you could take your words back? I suspect most of us have been guilty of that on multiple occasions. What's even worse, we seem to have an uncanny ability to hurl words that hurt our spouses most because we know the spots where they're sensitive or vulnerable.

Rage can cause so much damage in a marriage. Words spoken in anger can seep into our souls, wounding us deeply. The next time we're in those situations, we'd be wise to practice quietness until we get ourselves under control. Stop and pray and ask God to make your attitude right before you say angry words that could be remembered forever.

Do you have a problem with anger?
How does that impact your relationship?

Careful Words

> "By your words you will be justified,
> and by your words you will be condemned."
> MATTHEW 12:37 ESV

At first glance, these words sound like they rolled off the lips of a stern judge. Actually, they were spoken by Jesus to the Pharisees in response to a severe criticism they made concerning the source of Jesus' healing power.

Our words do matter. More than that, words reveal our motives and our heart. Not the carefully crafted responses we give, but rather the words that tumble out of our mouths, unbidden. Like a pop quiz in school, caught off-guard, we hear ourselves saying things we never planned on saying or even thought we were capable of saying. These circumstances reveal our true heart. The Holy Spirit allows it, not to embarrass us, but to change us. We only seek change if we acknowledge we need it.

Do you have the courage to ask God
to reveal your heart to you?
Have you or your spouse ever said anything
that surprised both of you?

Each Has a Gift

If your gift is to encourage others, be encouraging.
If it is giving, give generously.
If God has given you leadership ability, take the responsibility seriously.
And if you have a gift for showing kindness to others, do it gladly.

ROMANS 12:8 NLT

We were not all designed to be replications of each other. Our Father is wonderfully creative, and he loves displaying it. Each of us have been given different gifts to use in service to one another. Any time a believer has a God-given talent or skill, the Bible makes it clear that the purpose of it is not for the elevation of the individual but the betterment of the church body.

Using our gifts take practice and faith. It is God alone who can cause new life and growth, but we must be faithful to step out and use what he has trusted us with. If we do not use our gifts, they will rust, and he will call someone else instead. If we use our gifts to only serve our own purposes, all our gain is for naught. Sometimes recognizing our gifts take a level of self-awareness that we have not yet reached. Other people, especially our spouses who know us intimately, can help us identify our gifts and encourage us to use them properly. We also ought to encourage our spouses to embrace their gifts and support them as they learn to use them.

What gifts have you been given?
What gifts does your spouse have?
How can you use them to help others?

Good Steps

Follow the steps of the good,
and stay on the paths of the righteous.
For only the godly will live in the land,
and those with integrity will remain in it.

PROVERBS 2:20-21 NLT

In a world saturated with corruption and sensuality, it is difficult to stay on the path of the righteous. Everywhere we turn there are evil ploys endeavoring to draw us down to death. Sin is not life-giving. The enemy lies and promises happiness, but it is fleeting and leads only to death—a numbing of our conscience, a deafness to God's voice, and spiritual decay. If we do not turn from our wicked tendencies and follow the steps of the good, we will continue further down a path that is difficult to come back from.

Those who stay committed to the commandments of the Lord, who get back up and try harder when they fall, and who humbly request mercy and help from the Lord will inherit the Promised Land. When Jehovah bequeathed the Promised Land to his faithful followers, it was a literal land that also stood as a figurative future telling of his eternal kingdom. Solomon explains that maintaining our integrity is rewarded by God in the form of residency in his heavenly home. That is definitely a worthwhile reward!

What can you do when you take a step in the wrong direction?

May

Love does not demand its own way.
It is not irritable,
and it keeps no record of being wronged.

1 CORINTHIANS 13:5 NLT

Growing in Love

The LORD longs to be gracious to you;
therefore he will rise up to show you compassion.
For the LORD is a God of justice.
Blessed are all who wait for him!

ISAIAH 30:18 NIV

Oh, how the Lord longs to show his great love to us. With compassion and mercy he gently exhorts us to do what is right. God is not a harsh taskmaster. Using his example, learn to delight in each other, showing gentleness, grace, and tenderness especially in times of pressure. Strive to treat your spouse with warmth and affection. Be sure not to keep score or hold grudges.

God does not judge you for your faults; shouldn't you do the same for the one you love? A sure way to improve the bond of love you share is to treat your spouse better than you are treated. There can only be improvement. Celebrate the blessings you share, compliment each other, treat one another with tenderness and forgiveness. Your marriage will be better for it!

Are you quick to forgive or do you hold on to grudges?
Can you think of one specific compliment for your spouse?
Can you purpose to be more kind?

Winning Teams

May the God of endurance and encouragement grant you to live in such harmony with one another, in accord with Christ Jesus, that together you may with one voice glorify the God and Father of our Lord Jesus Christ.

ROMANS 15:5-6 ESV

The purpose of our lives is for the praise and glory of God, and we truly feel an overwhelming sense of satisfied accomplishment when we are living the way we were created to live. The best way to do that, however, is not alone. We are meant to serve each other and to serve God together. The metaphor Paul uses to describe this unity is one voice in harmony. Within a harmony are different parts. By his brilliant design, God created each of us with separate skills and abilities but with the same calling to praise him.

We work best when we allow each person to operate within their range but still adjust our voices so we can harmonize together. We each have a different part to sing, but we are still singing together and ought to remember that. This is neither a song to us nor about us. Our lives are meant to be a form of worship to the Almighty Maker who gave us life and a voice. Showing grace and adjusting our pitch for the sake of others around us blesses the heart of God and beautifully unites us as a family.

How have you and your spouse learned to harmonize?
How do you serve God differently but still together?

Keep Romance Alive

Your love delights me, my treasure, my bride.
Your love is better than wine,
your perfume more fragrant than spices.
SONG OF SOLOMON 4:10 NLT

It is such a gift from God to view our marriage in light of how King Solomon viewed his bride. This book is in the Bible for marriages! Song of Solomon shows us how to view our love for our spouses differently than many—maybe most—marriages in the world. We have the choice of cherishing our relationship with our spouses over everything except our relationship with God.

As we delve into God's Word, our hearts are opened and warmed toward our spouse. We can see the gifts that God has blessed them with, the characteristics that honor him, and the traits that are revealed only through intimacy. King Solomon basks in the love of his bride, and we also can cherish and enjoy the love of our spouse. As we turn our eyes upon God, the opportunity for a deep, soul-inspiring relationship within our marriage is right there. The Lord intends for us to cherish and seek our spouses more than we long for the luxuries of this world.

Do you choose your husband or wife over all other people, all luxuries in life, and all beautiful things that pass through your day?

Like Jesus

In your relationships with one another, have the same mindset as Christ Jesus: Who, being in very nature God, did not consider equality with God something to be used to his own advantage; rather, he made himself nothing by taking the very nature of a servant, being made in human likeness…he humbled himself by becoming obedient to death.

PHILIPPIANS 2:5-8 NIV

The King of the universe chose to come humbly to this world which he had created in the form of a servant. He could have arrived in all his power and demanded that we serve him, but instead he showed us compassion and came to teach us how to serve others. He washed feet, ate with sinners, preached until he was exhausted, healed the sick, and even gave his own life. He taught us how to love and how to live sacrificially.

The world will be able to identify followers of Jesus by the love they show to other people. We have a lot of love to give because God first gave it to us. Instead of status, we should aim to pursue servanthood.

How can you use what you have been given to serve your spouse and others?

Peace in Humility

Humble yourselves under the mighty power of God,
and at the right time he will lift you up in honor.
Give all your worries and cares to God, for he cares about you.

1 PETER 5:6-7 NLT

We all crave significance and recognition. We long to be honored, and that desire is not wrong. It is the way God created us. When it becomes a problem is when it distracts us from honoring and glorifying God because we become engrossed with serving ourselves and getting credit for what we have done. God instructs us to be humble. In truth, simply understanding the majesty of God should be enough to humble any of us!

God promises to lift us up and honor us in the right way. He knows that desire is in us because he created us, but he wants to be the one to give that recognition and approval. By searching for it from others we only deprive ourselves of the real deal, which can only come from God. The praises of men and women will never satisfy the desire for approval in our soul.

Do you trust that God is more than enough
to fill your heart and satisfy your soul?

Heavenly Songs

"Worthy are you to take the book and to break its seals;
for you were slain, and purchased for God with your blood men
from every tribe and tongue and people and nation."

REVELATION 5:9 NASB

John wept as he realized the depth of his sin—of humanity's sin. We could not cover the cost of our depravities fully, for we all fell short of the righteousness required. Death was imminent. Then, in an allegorical taking of the scroll and opening of its seals, the perfect and pure Christ paid the ransom for our sins and redeemed the entire world from death. Now, rather than weeping, there was great rejoicing! A new song broke out across heaven as all of creation praised the Worthy Lamb for the salvation he had brought.

The holiness and importance of this act can never be overlooked. Every nation on the planet received grace that day; it is ours to accept. Never allow the enemy to whisper lies in your ears about limited grace or try to fool you into believing you are somehow unworthy of God's love. Indeed, you were unworthy, and Christ stood in your place. You are now completely accepted, fully purified, and an heir of the kingdom of God.

Does the weight of your sin bring you to your knees?
Can you fathom Christ's forgiveness
and rise up in that freedom?

Not Where but How

"A time is coming and has now come when the true worshipers will worship the Father in the Spirit and in truth, for they are the kind of worshipers the Father seeks. God is spirit, and his worshipers must worship in the Spirit and in truth."

JOHN 4:23-24 NIV

While speaking with Jesus, it became apparent to the Samaritan woman that he was aware of her sinful lifestyle and she quickly shifted the conversation to the topic of worship. Where should worship take place: on the mountain where they stood or in Jerusalem? Of course, Jesus knew her heart and loved her despite her brokenness. He meets each of us where we are, and he addresses the conditions of our hearts before even turning to our sinful symptoms.

Jesus usually asked a very direct question to whomever he was addressing that cut right to the matter mulling in their minds. For the Samaritan woman, who had been through a series of relationships and never found the love she was so desperate for, Jesus promised her that if she drank the water he offered, she would never thirst again. He answered her question of worship by explaining that worship starts in the heart. We don't need to be in a physical place to worship God but in an honest place within our hearts of truly seeking him.

How does God meet you where you are?

Grace Agents

Be alert and of sober mind. Your enemy the devil prowls around like a roaring lion looking for someone to devour. Resist him, standing firm in the faith, because you know that the family of believers throughout the world is undergoing the same kind of suffering.

1 PETER 5:8-9 NIV

*O*ur gift of salvation does not mean the elimination of pain. In this life, we are guaranteed to have troubles. We will face hardships, and many will face persecution. This is not an indication of lack of love or care from God. On the contrary, we are sharing in the suffering of Christ, just as we will share in his eternal glory. God has made us co-heirs of his kingdom with Christ Jesus, and that means that we each have our own cross to bear. It is by his kindness that we have been called to shine the light of Jesus in the darkness, and with the darkness comes deep depravity.

Corruption and wickedness should not intimidate us or silence our message because we have a promise from God that he will always uphold us. When our lives are over, we will be invited into the eternal glory reserved for us because of God's great kindness. One day, all our pain and suffering will be over, but until that day comes, we press on because of our connection with Jesus.

How does suffering benefit your relationship with God?

Love

Love is not rude, is not selfish, does not get upset with others.
Love does not count up wrongs that have been done.

1 CORINTHIANS 13:5 NCV

The love we have to give is greater than what is produced in this world because our love comes from the Father who so abundantly poured himself out for us. Because we have experienced the kindness of God, we can lean into that and rise above being rude to others. Selfishness seems petty and pointless when we have been given so much grace and so many blessings.

It is easy to become upset with people, especially our spouses, because they are bound to disappoint us from time to time. Real, godly love covers those feelings of annoyance with patience and peace that help us resist our natural urges. Praise God that he does not keep a record of the wrong things we have done! We ought to extend the same pardon to others. The love of God demands that we do not count the wrongs of others. He has shown us the way to love, and he has given us the strength and compassion to walk in the same manner.

*How can you avoid unloving reactions in your marriage
and lean on the love of God instead?*

Sprouting Seeds

Do not be children in your thinking.
Be infants in evil, but in your thinking be mature.

1 CORINTHIANS 14:20 ESV

There is something very rewarding in watching what we plant grow. Just as parents raise children to become responsible adults, God intends for his children to grow spiritually. Many Christians are content with only the seed of God's Word; this verse challenges us to grow. As we grow in knowing and loving him, he invites us to be a part of what he is doing. He equips us for tasks he knew we would undertake.

God intends for your marriage to be a growing relationship, full of joy and satisfaction. Knowing him means understanding that he has a purpose for your life and marriage. The more you grow in him, the greater the blessings life brings.

Is your marriage growing?
What are you doing to make sure that growth continues?
Are you discovering God's purpose for your marriage?
Are you seeking to know him more intimately?

Confident Hope

Faith is the confidence in what we hope for
and assurance about what we do not see.

HEBREWS 11:1 NIV

We have been called to have faith in what we do not see, but not in what we do not know. Our heavenly Father has proven himself faithful and true to his promises. His words have been established time and time again, and never in all of history has he forsaken his elect. It is our joy and honor to follow him into an unseen future, but we don't follow blindly because we know in whom we place our faith.

The hope that we have is not a simple wish that things will happen as the Bible predicts. We are completely persuaded without doubt that everything will happen exactly as God promised. Faith in God is not a gamble or a dart thrown in the dark because he has made himself known to his people. Our faith is the unquestionable confidence we have that he is holy and dependable and will continue to lead us in the way that is right.

How does faith require active obedience?

Make Music

Be filled with the Spirit, speaking to one another with psalms, hymns, and songs from the Spirit. Sing and make music from your heart to the Lord.

EPHESIANS 5:18-19 NIV

As a stark opposite example of being drunk or "filled with wine," Paul told Christians to be filled with the Spirit. Instead of being controlled by our own intoxication, we should give control of ourselves and our lives to the Lord. His Spirit fills us, guides us, and guards us.

In response to being filled with the Spirit and with the joy that accompanies that, Paul noted different forms of worship and praise. Although there were several separate styles mentioned, the focal point of all of them was the Lord. Christians enjoy many different genres of music. If the purpose is to worship God and our hearts are filled with joy and love for the Lord and others, then we should not get caught up on the style of the song. God cares more about the conditions of our hearts.

How do you prefer to worship the Lord?
What style of music encourages your heart?

Captive Thoughts

Don't copy the behavior and customs of this world, but let God transform
you into a new person by changing the way you think. Then you will learn
to know God's will for you, which is good and pleasing and perfect.

ROMANS 12:2 NLT

*I*nstead of approaching life asking, "What do I want?" or, "What is
the best thing for me?" we should abide by the question, "What does
God want of me?" We were, after all, created to worship our Creator
and there is nothing more fulfilling or exhilarating than that. This
world and its pleasures fight for our attention, but their promises
are empty. Living for ourselves accomplishes nothing noteworthy or
eternal and it certainly doesn't honor our spouses.

The behaviors of this world are vulgar and narcistic; we ought not
copy those. By allowing God to transform our minds, by opening
our hearts to hear his truth and recognize the lies we previously
believed, we start to resemble him more and the world less.
Eventually, we will look out of place here, but that is because we have
modeled our lifestyles after an eternal kingdom with heavenly values
that will never fail or pass away.

*What is an example of a commonplace,
worldly custom that is contrary to a godly lifestyle?*

Fruit of Kindness

Praise the LORD, for he has shown me the wonders of his unfailing love.
He kept me safe when my city was under attack.

PSALM 31:21 NLT

*I*f there were ever a book to encourage and uplift us, the Psalms would be the place to turn. It declares God's goodness, often during times of significant distress, and offers hope in the Lord no matter how dire life may seem. There were so many times King David found himself in a rut or a jam and he needed divine help. As testified in this verse, God came through for him, and he will come through for us. His answers are not always what we expect them to be, and sometimes the wonder of his love is simply that his presence is with us to help and guide us, but even that is miraculous.

The God of the universe is on our side, and he never leaves us to fight alone. He was with David in the city under siege, and he is with us through every one of life's difficulties as well. He is involved in our marriages, our struggles, our relationships, and our futures. No matter what attacks may befall us, big or small, he is with us, showing the wonders of his love.

*Do you actively involve God
in the different elements of your life?*

Heavenly Comfort

I truly believe I will live to see the LORD's goodness.
Wait for the LORD's help. Be strong and brave,
and wait for the LORD's help.

PSALM 27:13-14 NCV

As children, we sought out our mother or father for comfort when we were hurt. A hug, soft words, a bandage, and a kiss on a boo-boo brought comfort and contentment. The pain might have still been there but we felt secure and loved. What a wonderful feeling that was.

Where do we go when we are hurt, afraid, or stressed now? What do we do when we feel unsure, mentally beat down, or anxious. Sharing your worries with your spouse is a good first step. It really is true that "a burden shared is a burden halved." Even better is sharing your hurts with the Lord. God has promised to help us shoulder our problems. Have faith that he will help. Praying with your spouse on a regular basis can help establish a dependence on the Lord for help when life gets tough. The love-bond between the two of you will be strengthened as you seek God's comfort through prayer.

Do the two of you make time to pray together?
How do you share your worries and concerns with your spouse?
Are you comfortable praying together
or would you rather pray alone?

Sleep in Peace

I go to bed and sleep in peace,
because, LORD, only you keep me safe.
PSALM 4:8 NCV

*D*avid often had to hide for his life; he had seen battles, and he had made mistakes. There was always uncertainty and danger in his life, yet the one thing he was certain about was that his God loved him and would always be watching out for him. In his heart he had the peace of God, so he was able to unplug from the day's drama and sleep soundly.

Peter offered a perfect example of resting in the promises of God. James had just been killed, Peter was in prison chained between two guards, and Herod planned to execute Peter the next day. Even with his looming doom, the uncomfortable conditions, and the tragic news of his friend, Peter's faith was fully in his Father. He slept so soundly, in fact, that when an angel came to free him, he had to smack him on the side in order to wake him up (Acts 12:7)! Give the day's cares to God and rest in the knowledge that no matter what happens your Father will always be there for you, keeping you safe.

Where does your safety lie?

Distinctly Unique

"I will make him a helper fit for him."

GENESIS 2:18 ESV

Marriages are all different. Why? Because each marriage is made up of two distinctly unique people. Some couples spend most of their time together and some are only able to catch up a little bit each day or on the weekends. Depending on what stage of life you are in, togetherness will greatly vary.

Know that while your marriage may not look like other marriages, God has put you together. Your relationship is a good thing. You complement each other. Find ways to spend more time together. Develop the common interests you share. If you can't think of anything you both like, try new activities. Be creative. Make time for enjoying each other's company.

Are you comfortable with each other?
What do you do together that you both find fun?
Are you willing to carve out time
to spend with just the two of you?

Blessed

Blessed is the man who walks not in the counsel of the wicked,
nor stands in the way of sinners, nor sits in the seat of scoffers;
but his delight is in the law of the LORD,
and on his law he meditates day and night.

PSALM 1:1-2 ESV

The downhill trajectory of this psalm is a warning to not even begin to go toward sin. It may start with simply walking among the wicked, but then it transitions into standing the way they do and finally joining them by sitting in their seat. The more we immerse ourselves in unrighteous behavior and align with those who scoff at what is virtuous, the more we begin to take on their features. Soon, we appear just as they do, and not long after that, we have fully joined them in their wickedness.

The person who avoids this slippery slope will experience blessings from the Lord. A rational result of refusing to participate in regrettable acts is that regrets are evaded. Rather than sin, we ought to delight in the Word of God. There is great joy and revelation found within its texts which bring delight and further blessings to the reader. Day and night it should be before us so we can learn to walk the way it teaches us to and discover the Lord's astounding blessings.

What have you read in the Bible recently that delighted you?

Together in Grief

"Blessed are the poor in spirit, for theirs is the kingdom of heaven.
Blessed are those who mourn, for they will be comforted."

MATTHEW 5:3-4 NIV

Jesus was not addressing financial standings in this beatitude. To be poor in spirit means being humble enough to recognize the depravity of our own human condition and dependent on God. It is the opposite of arrogance or having a sense of being spiritually superior or self-sustained. Those who are poor in spirit recognize they are undeserving of acceptance in the kingdom of heaven, yet it is this exact meek mindset that grants them entrance, since they request it of God rather than assuming it for themselves.

Similarly, those who mourn do so out of a contrite and broken heart. Their mourning may be a result of sin they have committed, sin committed against them, or simply living in a fallen world which is under the dominion of death. Whatever the case, with the kingdom of God comes an end to sin and death, and so their mourning will be no more. To be *blessed* is much deeper than just being happy. Clearly those who mourn are not happy, but they are still blessed because they have been given a promise that their mourning will end.

When your spouse is grieving, how can you offer comfort?
How is this considered kingdom work?

Be an Encourager

Encourage one another and build one another up,
just as you are doing.

1 THESSALONIANS 5:11 NASB

The context of this message is based on the end of the world. Paul recognized that the believers in Thessalonica were doing a praiseworthy job at encouraging each other, and so he commissioned them to keep going. This mandate is as applicable and essential now as ever. Even when the world gets rocky and the future is uncertain, it is our obligation to build one another up because this present life does not dictate our future hope in Jesus Christ.

The very understanding that we will be spending eternity with our loving Creator is motivation enough to reach out to other believers and reassure them of the promises we have received. When we turn on the news and see the headlines, we should not become dismayed because we know what awaits us at the end of the age. Together we should focus on serving the Lord and equipping each other. The powers of earth will taunt us and try to demoralize us, but we stand on the truth of the Word of God, and we cling to his promises for strength.

How can you encourage and build up your spouse today?

Love Always

Love bears all things, believes all things,
hopes all things, endures all things.

1 CORINTHIANS 13:7 ESV

While reading through the love passage of 1 Corinthians 13, it becomes apparent that the true nature of love puts the needs of others first. Love lays itself down for the sake of others. This is the kind of love Jesus demonstrated for us, and it's the love we are supposed to have for each other. Love does not quit when times are tough or relationships are difficult; it bears all things. This does not mean we need to subject ourselves to injury or insult, but we are also not supposed to return hate for hate. Perhaps we remove ourselves from the destructive circumstances, but we still bear the weight of love and we never give up.

Love believes all things: not in a naive sense but in a way that validates others and creates a safe place of vulnerability and trust. If someone is lying, that is between them and God and they must carry their own sin. The dishonesty is not ours to bear or meddle in, we only need to show love and acceptance. Those who have known the love of Christ know also how to secure their hope in him. This helps us in the midst of hard times to endure all things in the name of love.

*What can you do to put the needs
of your spouse before your own today?*

The Golden Rule

"Do to others as you would have them do to you."

LUKE 6:31 NIV

This is a straightforward verse yet heavy with meaning. These words are at the heart of the Christian message: to love others as yourself. It is fondly known as the Golden Rule. Most of us strive to take really good care of ourselves and at least are aware when something is wrong. Most people first and foremost consider their own needs, wants, gains, and success. However, as Christians we are told to consider the needs of others first and do to them what we would wish to have done to us.

Self-centeredness is contrary to love, and it creeps in when we become too inward focused. The example Christ set for us demonstrates incredible selflessness that goes beyond human expectation or reason. Despite the contempt he was shown by the people he came to save, Christ sacrificed his own body to save our souls. It behooves us, therefore, to joyfully go the extra mile in loving our neighbor, spouse, sibling, stranger, parent, or whomever needs our care. We are told to love as we love ourselves which takes effort and discipline in a world that glamorizes self-idolization.

What does it look like in daily life to love and care for your spouse the way you want to be loved and cared for?

A God Decision

I will instruct you and teach you in the way you should go;
I will counsel you with my loving eye on you.

PSALM 32:8 NIV

The mysteries of God are many. So great is his love for us. In his wisdom, he chooses to reveal his answers and intentions at the right time. We love to be known and understood by each other, and in the same way God loves to be known and understood by us. In his caring, paternal way, he divulges secrets if we only take time to listen. The path to life he has made known to us, and he teaches us his ways as a Father teaches his children.

Anyone who has opened their heart to receive the Lord's lessons will receive them, and their understanding will increase. He does not hide his face from us but keeps his gaze upon us because we are his beloved creation. It is by his counsel through his Word that we learn the best ways in which to live. He is a good teacher and the best mentor; he walks together with us so we will not go astray. There exists no other leader as great as our King, and he will rule and reign forever!

What has the Lord been teaching you recently?

Serving Together

I have been a constant example of how you can help those in need
by working hard. You should remember the words of the Lord Jesus:
"It is more blessed to give than to receive."

ACTS 20:35 NLT

We have been charged by God to be generous. We can support our church endeavors, missionaries, various service charities and the like. We can help our neighbors in time of need, providing meals or transportation. We can be generous with our time, assisting others with the talents the Lord has given to each of us. We can act as mentors, coaches, leaders, Sunday school teachers, community garden helpers, or small group leaders. Why not find something that the two of you can do together. The time you spend in a common activity can enhance your marriage.

If you donate money to causes, be sure to involve your spouse. Discuss and decide monetary gifts before they are given. If one of you is volunteering a large time commitment, be sure to talk it over together. Your first commitment is to your spouse, but the two of you will find blessing in your kind generosity.

Are you generous with what God has blessed you with?
Do you have talents you aren't sharing?
What plan for charity or service can you try?

Gratitude Always

Giving thanks always for all things unto God and the Father
in the name of our Lord Jesus Christ.

EPHESIANS 5:20 KJV

The type of thankfulness Paul describes here is not a one-time act of appreciation but a lifestyle of thanksgiving. By giving thanks always, we constantly remember the grace we have been shown, and our gratitude pours out into all corners of our lives. Someone who appreciates life and feels grateful will act differently. They care about the needs of others, they are not constantly pushing to get their fair share of everything, and they are generally more pleasant to be around.

Thanksgiving creates a positive countenance, welcoming disposition, and a gracious attitude toward others. People who are thankful are not as easily put off by life's trivial upsets because they do not believe they are owed anything. They recognize the incredible gifts of love and mercy they have already received, and their lives are a living tribute to the God who gave them all good things.

What are you grateful for?
How does your life show it?

Morning Conversations

LORD, every morning you hear my voice.
Every morning, I tell you what I need,
and I wait for your answer.

PSALM 5:3 NCV

When David went before God in prayer every morning, he did so with confidence that God heard him and would answer. Our prayers are not empty one-way conversations. They are not simply symbolic gestures of spiritualism. When we pray, we are talking directly to the almighty maker of heaven and earth, and he hears us.

Our Father listens to our prayers, knows our needs, and answers us. His answers are not always what we would like or were expecting, but they are guaranteed to be completely based out of love and wisdom. The Lord has a far better vantagepoint than we do and he understands the bigger picture of our lives and of all humanity. We can go directly before our King with prayers and petitions in full confidence because we serve a caring and compassionate God who desires more than servanthood. He wants an open and honest relationship with us and even calls us his friends.

Do you take time every morning to pray to God?
Do you leave time to pause and listen for a response?
What are some ways you have seen God respond to your prayers?

Happy Days

There is a time to cry and a time to laugh.
There is a time to be sad and a time to dance.
ECCLESIASTES 3:4 NCV

It is easy to recognize that there are times of sorrow and times of happiness. The Lord himself cries and laughs. It takes courage to be able to express these pivotal emotions, and yet both are important in certain seasons. Sometimes life deals us heartache and denying how we feel so we can continue as if nothing happened can be harmful. It is often the Lord's intent to lead us through the hard times not around them. Doing so increases our faith and opens our eyes to our utter dependency on him. He is prepared to be our Comforter, but we first need to admit that we need his comfort.

After the dark night, there comes an appropriate time to lay our sadness before the Lord and rise again. This does not mean we must simply stop feeling, but that we refuse to let the pain keep us down or stop us from following the Lord. To embrace laughing and dancing again is not denying the tragic times but making the choice to press forward in the comfort and love of God.

Are you in a season of laughing or crying?
Are you comfortable being where God has you?

Rejoice Always

Rejoice in the Lord always.
I will say it again: Rejoice!
PHILIPPIANS 4:4 NIV

Joy is a great gift that God has given to his followers. Joy is far more powerful than happiness because it does not diminish due to circumstances. The type of joy that God gives does not come from this world; therefore, it is not dependent on this world. No enemy can steal it and no disappointment can drown it out. It should define our personalities and be ever in our hearts. Paul wrote this letter to the church in Philippi while he was in prison in Rome. He had endured numerous hardships on his way to Rome, then once he arrived, he was wrongly accused and arrested. Still, he chose to rejoice in the Lord because he knew how great God's love for him was.

Understanding what God has done for us will fill us with joy and it will be obvious to those around us. Having a real relationship with Jesus Christ does not mean that we praise him with our mouths on Sunday mornings but that our entire disposition every day is one of rejoicing in the fact that we have been redeemed. Even when we are sad, that joy is still in our hearts and it compels us forward.

Why do you think this commandment
was so important that Paul repeated it?
What does rejoicing in the Lord do for a person?

Steadfast Love

Let not steadfast love and faithfulness forsake you;
bind them around your neck;
write them on the tablet of your heart.

PROVERBS 3:3 ESV

When you made a marriage covenant before God, you promised love and loyalty to your spouse. Marriage is a picture of God's commitment to us, so we also accept the mantle of representing this reflection to the watching world. The word for steadfast love that Solomon used while writing this proverb is the Hebrew word *he'sed* which means "loyalty to one's covenant." When we make a covenant either to God or to our spouse, it is binding. It is to be etched into our hearts.

Sometimes marriages are dismantled because we live in a fallen world where sin exists, but as far as we can while still faithfully following God, our covenants need to be loyally upheld. Our God is forever faithful to us and he teaches us to be like him. He will never abandon us, and we know his words are true. As we cling to steadfast love and faithfulness, we are strengthened in our commitments by knowing that the Lord is committed to us.

Practically speaking, what does it mean to bind your commitment to love and faithfulness around your neck, or to write it on your heart?

Letting Go

Those who do right will continue to do right,
and those whose hands are not dirty with sin will grow stronger.
JOB 17:9 NCV

The past can haunt a marriage; forgiveness can bring freedom and delight. When you confess your transgressions to the Lord there is mercy, grace, and forgiveness. Sins are forgotten and you have a clean slate. Justification in the eyes of the Lord is a gift. Learn from your misdeeds and strive to do right. What freedom and independence comes from confession and forgiveness!

Bringing up the past can bring destruction to the joy in your marriage. God has declared confessed sin to be banished "as far as the east is to the west." Move forward with each other, start every day new and fresh. If your husband or wife has disappointed you in the past, give them the benefit of your love and God's trust in them. Help them to continue to do the right thing by building them up and not tearing them down. Treat each other with respect and love.

Can you be encouraging to your spouse?
Do you bring up the past when you have arguments?
How can you let go and move forward?

Devoted to Prayer

Devote yourselves to prayer,
keeping alert in it with an attitude of thanksgiving.

COLOSSIANS 4:2 NASB

How do you pray? On your knees, in your car, running after your toddler, on a picnic, while you fix the fence? Do you sing praise songs along with the radio, ask God's forgiveness with tears streaming down your face? All of these encompass what it is to pray. The Lord desires a relationship with us that is deep and personal. It is by sharing our thoughts, our thanks, and our innermost desires with him that true relationship forms. Petition or requesting from God is certainly one form of prayer but so is praising the Lord for his grace and mercy.

Together you can seek wisdom and solutions. Prayer can take practice. Make it a habit. When the two of you met it took time to get to know one another. You shared your past, your hopes and dreams, and your future plans. God loves you and wants to hear these things too. Approach prayer as a conversation, an expression of thanks, and acknowledgement of all God has done for you.

Are you comfortable in prayer?
What have you heard from God recently?
Do you pray together?

June

Above all, constantly echo
God's intense love for one another,
for love will be a canopy
over a multitude of sins.

1 PETER 4:8 TPT

Rest in Love

The LORD your God is with you;
The mighty One will save you.
He will rejoice over you.
You will rest in his love;
he will sing and be joyful about you.

ZEPHANIAH 3:17 NCV

The prophet Zephaniah speaks lucidly of restoration. Out of our deeply ingrained fear, the condemnations and doubts, the brokenness and arrogance, God takes us as victorious warriors, bringing us into joyful relationship with him. Somehow, he does more than bail us out from mistakes and insufficient efforts: He rejoices over us. He turns away his judgments, being quiet in his love.

Our depravity and weakness are not enough to drive our compassionate, powerful Savior away. We remain forever in the quarry of his love. Our marriages should reflect this love between God and his people. We should rejoice over each other with shouts of joy and endeavor to pursue each other with a conviction so strong only God could provide it. This will be our witness to the brokenhearted and unsaved. What kind of apathy can overcome the unfading love of God?

How do you rest in God's love?
How can you show the same kind of love to your spouse?

Honored

"Honor your father and mother.
Love your neighbor as yourself."
MATTHEW 19:19 NLT

*P*erhaps you are out with the guys, and they start talking unkindly about their wives or making comments about other women. Maybe girls' night turns into complaint night. Respect doesn't only apply when you are with your spouse. It means representing and protecting your spouse even when you are with others. Your neighbors, coworkers, and friends are watching. Your children need to see you respect each other, so they respect you and their future spouses.

Speak kindly, encourage, and value each other. Let your spouse know how important he or she is to you. This will bless your spouse, your relationship, and your home, and it will honor the Lord.

Why is respect so important in a relationship?
If you are in a situation like the ones above,
what can you do to honor and respect your spouse?
What are ways you can show respect for each other this week?

The Team

We are both God's workers.
And you are God's field, God's building.
1 CORINTHIANS 3:9 ESV

Rather than arguing over how ministry should be completed, Paul urged the Corinthian Christians to work together and model themselves after the example of Christ. Just like laborers in a field, some need to weed, some till, some plant, some water, and some harvest. These are all necessary yet different tasks. We will all do ministry differently. As the Spirit of God leads us and the Word of God directs us, we will engage in his work according to how he created us. We should not compare ourselves to others because each of us were made unique.

In the end, only God can cause plants to grow; only he can bring an increase. The field is big, and we cannot tend to it all ourselves. Rather than criticizing the way someone else does ministry, we should be praying that the Lord sends more people to help. We need to stop attempting to control ministers and ministry methods and start humbly working for God. We are a team, a family, and he is in control.

*How difficult is it for you to accept other people
doing things differently than you?
How can you make room for those differences?*

Best Consultant

Trust in the LORD with all your heart
and do not lean on your own understanding.
PROVERBS 3:5 NASB

The point of King Solomon's message was not to promote ignorance or discourage sound reasoning but to caution us that even the most intelligent of human understanding is fallible and subject to bias. Any of us can be misled because we do not have the full picture the way God does. Blind faith does not require us to stumble forward in the dark, uncertain of whether God will catch us or not. We can with certainty trust the Lord because he has given us more than substantial evidence that he is faithful and worthy of our confidence. His track record is flawless.

Leaning on God is much safer than leaning on our own understanding. At times he may ask us to do unorthodox things, but we know that his way is better than ours; his perspective is full while ours is partial, and his promises are sure even if ours are not. When God's call contradicts what we think we know, it is always best to trust him.

What do you have a difficult time trusting God with?

The Best Promise

"If I go and prepare a place for you,
I will come back and take you to be with me
that you also may be where I am."

JOHN 14:3 NIV

This world is not our ultimate destination, so our investments here should consider their eternal worth. We do not exist for this life alone but for the hope of an eternal home with Jesus. Although our intention may be to live intentionally and offer praise to God while here on earth, it is easy to succumb to the temptations and distractions we are constantly inundated with.

We must regularly remind ourselves of our true nature and calling. As children of the King, we were created for his kingdom and not simply this temporary dominion. Our treasures are not found here, for they are securely reserved with the Father. Even our hopes and dreams should not be wasted on present passing pleasures, for our eyes are focused forward to that wonderous moment when Christ returns for us. On that day, every eternal investment will be realized, and all other pursuits will perish.

How can you help remind your spouse
of their true nature and calling?

Brook of Bliss

The LORD is my shepherd; I shall not want.
He makes me lie down in green pastures.
He leads me beside still waters.
He restores my soul.
He leads me in paths of righteousness for his name's sake.

PSALM 23:1-3 ESV

As a former shepherd, King David understood the importance of a shepherd to the life of a sheep. Without a shepherd, sheep are vulnerable to all the elements and dangers of the wild. Even finding food and water would be a struggle without a kind and knowledgeable leader. A good shepherd offers protection, refreshment, and direction. David confidently declared that God was like a good shepherd and he lacked nothing under God's watchful care.

We choose to walk in righteousness, but God establishes our paths and helps us every step of the way. When we stumble, he brings restoration. When we get lost, he comes and finds us again. In his care, we are safe from all threats of danger. We find peace and contentment when we follow him and submit ourselves to his watchful gaze.

What happens to your peace and contentment
when you start to pursue other pleasures in life
at the expense of your relationship with God?

Covenant of Love

Know therefore that the LORD your God is God; he is the faithful God,
keeping his covenant of love to a thousand generations of those who love
him and keep his commandments.

DEUTERONOMY 7:9 NIV

*V*ulnerability can be scary because it requires that we open our
hearts to the possibility of getting hurt or rejected. But in being
vulnerable, we also open our hearts to love and be loved. When
we get married, we open our hearts and lives and pray that our
vulnerability is protected not abused. There will always be times
when we disappoint each other, and we have to continue to learn
how to love from God.

With our heavenly Father, we never need to be afraid of
vulnerability. He won't let us down, he will not abandon us, and he
cherishes our efforts of obedience. His covenant of love is assured.
Our hearts are safe trusting in him because he will always be
faithful. He rewards obedience with blessings and pours out his love
on us. He does not owe us anything, and still he binds himself in a
love covenant with us.

Do you have an honest and vulnerable
relationship with your spouse?
How does God's love for you help you love your partner better?

Never Alone

Lord, even when your path takes me through
the valley of deepest darkness,
fear will never conquer me, for you already have!
You remain close to me and lead me through it all the way.
Your authority is my strength and my peace.
The comfort of your love takes away my fear.
I'll never be lonely, for you are near.

PSALM 23:4 TPT

An unstoppable sort of boldness springs forth in our hearts when we remember that evil no longer has a hold on us. God defeated sin and set us free. We are reminded to never be afraid when evil rises against us because although it may appear to be a daunting foe, it is powerless to cause us harm. The Holy Spirit lives in us and has ordained our steps.

When we place our trust completely in God, our lives are forever changed, and the alteration in how we live testifies clearly to others who know us. Let us be a witness to those who are afraid and lost that there is freedom in Jesus Christ. Submitting ourselves and our ways to his perfect plan guides us away from sin and darkness and into safety. We are no longer subject to anything but the Lord, for he is our protector.

When you are gripped with fear,
what promises can you cling to?

Shield of Salvation

You have also given me the shield of Your salvation;
Your gentleness has made me great.

2 SAMUEL 22:36 NKJV

*T*he word *gentleness* used in this verse comes from the Greek word *gnanvah* which is also commonly translated as *meekness*. It seems outlandish that meekness could make someone great, yet that is exactly what David claimed in this song he wrote after God rescued him from being murdered by King Saul. No matter what hardships David faced, he had faith that God would sustain him. He knew his best defense was not his strength, his sword, or even his sling; his protection came from the Almighty whose salvation was like a shield all around him.

As we pursue the Lord, it quickly becomes obvious that we have not chosen a life of ease. God will help us overcome, and he will even make us great if we learn to trust his gentle hand. He is our shield and our refuge, our defender and our ultimate judge. It is better to be in his watchful care than to erect every earthly security we can imagine.

What is greatness in regard to the kingdom of God?

Undivided

Teach me your way, LORD,
that I may rely on your faithfulness;
give me an undivided heart,
that I may fear your name.
PSALM 86:11 NIV

Reliance on God's goodness and a reverent fear of his power leads to a proper understanding of who he is. His ways are superior to ours, and it is to our detriment to forsake his laws in favor of our own self interests. Instead of depending on ourselves—our limited strength and flawed logic—we turn to the tried and true faithfulness of God. Our hearts should be undivided, otherwise we will be torn in different directions as we ineffectively attempt to serve two masters.

We must decide to follow either ourselves or God. Since he has proven to be far more dependable than we are, it would be foolish to give our allegiance to anyone or anything other than him. With undivided hearts and reverent fear, our own desires are cast aside and become less attractive over time. In exchange, we find unbroken faithfulness, timeless promises, love that supersedes everything, and a committed Father. Although we stumble, he is there to catch us and help us make the right decisions.

How can you and your spouse be undivided in your allegiance
to God and still successful in your tasks on earth?

Temple Work

"Be strong and courageous, and do the work.
Don't be afraid or discouraged, for the LORD God, my God, is with you.
He will not fail you or forsake you.
He will see to it that all work related to the Temple of the Lord is finished."

1 CHRONICLES 28:20 NLT

Just as David reminded his chosen workers not to become discouraged as they were doing the work of the Lord, we need to remember who we work for and find encouragement in that. On difficult, draining days when we have worked all day for our families with nothing tangible to show for it, we can remember that it is ultimately for the Lord that we labor. God no longer resides in a temple, but in the hearts of his faithful followers.

Whether we are serving our spouse, teaching our children, helping a friend, or obeying a boss, we are serving the Lord first. Whatever task God has given us to do, we can rest assured knowing that he has given us all the tools necessary to succeed: all the strength, patience, wisdom, and valor that is required. It is his work that he has invited us into, and he will see it to completion. Take courage; remember that God is with you and do the work!

What has the Lord tasked you with?
How are you working to build up your marriage?

Rooted in Christ

Blessed is the man who trusts in the LORD, and whose hope is the LORD.
For he shall be like a tree planted by the waters,
which spreads out its roots by the river,
and will not fear when heat comes;
But its leaf will be green, and will not be anxious in the year of drought,
nor will cease from yielding fruit.

JEREMIAH 17:7-8 NKJV

When you were little and everything seemed right with the world, trust was easy. As you grew, times became much more confusing. We all have fond memories of the early days of marriage when young love flourished. Later, debates and differences ensued, and you wondered if this marriage was a mistake. It didn't help when it seemed there were more bills at the end of the day than money in the bank, more chores than hands, or more harsh words than kind ones.

Perhaps you wonder if God is still the God you thought he was. Through pain and discouragement, you continue to grow when you are rooted in Christ. Be supporting branches for each other, and dig into God's Word and promises together.

Does fear creep in at uncertain times?
When the winds of life blow, are your roots deep enough
to keep you to keep you grounded?
Talk with each other about your fears.

Everlasting and Unfailing

"I have loved you with an everlasting love;
I have drawn you with unfailing kindness."

JEREMIAH 31:3 NIV

The Israelites often forsook God and ran after other idols or chose to serve themselves. They would be struck with persecution again and go running back home to the Lord. Time and time again, he received them back. Usually there were consequences for their poor decisions, but God never turns aside a contrite heart.

Our true repentance should not present only when we need help, but the Lord understands the weakness of humans and he continues to welcome us back into his arms. His unfailing kindness pursues us and saves us from ourselves. Like a loving and protective father, he cares about his wayward children and will do whatever it takes to bring them into the safety of his home. Even when our faith is weak, he will accept us if we humbly ask him to. He helps us to mature in faith and gives us ample amounts of grace. His love is everlasting and his compassion is certain.

Do you sometimes feel unworthy
to go to God after you have sinned?
Do you realize that you are always unworthy,
but he desires you anyway?

Pursued by Love

Why would I fear the future?
For your goodness and love pursue me all the days of my life.
Then afterward, when my life is through,
I'll return to your glorious presence to be forever with you!

PSALM 23:6 TPT

*E*very day of our lives, God has had his hand on us. Even now his love surrounds and protects us. He is dependable, consistent, and loving, and that will never change. We do not need to fear the future because we have seen the way the Almighty has cared for his people in the past, and we have heard his promises to care for his people in the future. His character is both trustworthy and constant, so our faith is sure.

Even after our lives end, God continues to take care of us and has prepared an eternal home for us within his kingdom. If the whole world was in turmoil, and everything we knew to be static was suddenly shaken, still he would remain immovable because he is greater than any force in the universe. All things good and loving originate with him. Our home and our rest are found in him because being in his arms is the safest place we know. We truly have nothing to fear.

What about the future frightens you?
How can you and your spouse rest
in God's immovable character?

Sharpening Iron

Iron sharpens iron,
so one man sharpens another.
PROVERBS 27:17 NASB

Most of us have a true desire to serve God, but it's easy to slip along the way, to lose sight of our goal to live for him. That's where having a spouse who also loves God is such a huge gift—because you can help each other with encouragement, accountability, and a commitment to work together to become who God wants you to be.

If we aren't where we need to be spiritually, we can be a deterrent to our spouses instead of a blessing. We can't help sharpen someone else if we haven't worked to become sharp ourselves. When iron sharpens iron, there has to be the touch of someone's hands for the sharpening process. That's where God comes in, and a wise couple will say, "Lord, sharpen us so that we can help sharpen each other."

How can you help sharpen each other?
Are you where you need to be spiritually?

Joyful Medicine

A joyful heart is good medicine,
but a crushed spirit dries up the bones.
PROVERBS 17:22 ESV

There is no doubt that God has the greatest sense of humor. Just look at his creation. Have you ever seen a platypus? Watched a giraffe pick up something from the ground? Witnessed a baby goat frolicking? Creating must have been an act of holy hilarity! Medical journals and research studies are full of the benefits of laughter. From heart health and lowered blood pressure to short term memory benefits, everything indicates the adage is true: *Laughter is good medicine.*

God's word goes deeper than the adage. True joy is a profound assurance in the character of God and his goodness toward his children. Joy frees us to rise above our circumstances and delight in our Creator. Life can be seriously tough, but a joyful heart recognizes happiness does not lie in our situation. Good humor lifts our souls.

Do you and your spouse take—and make—time to laugh?
What are some activities you can share together
to bring humor back into your routine?

Climates of Chaos

I heard a loud shout from the throne, saying, "Look, God's home is now among his people! He will live with them, and they will be his people. God himself will be with them. He will wipe every tear from their eyes, and there will be no more death or sorrow or crying or pain. All these things are gone forever."

REVELATION 21:3-4 NLT

Prior to Christ's sacrifice, sin separated people from God. Atonement had to be made for sins in the form of animal sacrifices, and people had to travel to the temple for their prayers and offerings. When Jesus came to fulfil the law and offer himself as the final and ultimate sacrifice, he explained that it was no longer necessary to travel to the temple to worship God. What mattered now was that those who worshipped him did so in spirit and in truth.

We have been given direct access to God through prayer. Although this is an astounding privilege, it is still far removed from the close relationship God shared with his people in the Garden of Eden and from what he desires to have with his people now. One day when we are finally called home to be with the Lord, we will have that kind of personal and intimate relationship with our Creator again. All death and sorrow will be cast out, and we will walk with God just like he intended from the beginning.

How can you take time now to focus on growing your relationship with Jesus?

Heavenly Peace

"Peace I leave with you; my peace I give you. I do not give to you as the world gives. Do not let your hearts be troubled and do not be afraid."

JOHN 14:27 NIV

Jesus spoke these words to his disciples in preparation of what he knew was about to happen. He was going to be arrested and crucified and his disciples—his closest friends—would scatter. They would feel lost and confused until Jesus returned to them from the dead, but even after that, he would leave them. His Spirit of peace would remain with them to help them because after his ascension they would undergo great persecution.

God does not leave us unprepared or alone, he always prepares us for what is coming and walks with us every step of the way. It is by his strength and because of his teachings that we can navigate our way through life. The world cannot offer us lasting peace, only passing pleasure. The peace Jesus gives fills us with courage and satisfaction. Our hearts are not troubled when we are walking with him. Nothing can fill us with fear when we are already filled with Christ's love.

Do you struggle with fear?
Why is fear the rival of love?

Teamwork

Yes, there are many parts, but only one body. The eye can never say to the
hand, "I don't need you." The head can't say to the feet, "I don't need you."
In fact, some parts of the body that seem weakest and least important are
actually the most necessary. So God has put the body together such that
extra honor and care are given to those parts that have less dignity.
This makes for harmony among the members, so that all the members
care for each other.

1 CORINTHIANS 12:20-21, 24-25 NLT

Before looking down on the work of someone else or issuing
excessive praise to those who have more esteemed roles, we should
remember that each of us depends on others just as if we were one
body. None of us can complete the work of the Lord alone, so unity
within the body of Christ is of utmost importance.

Harmony and respect should be primary traits of those professing
faith in Christ since it is he who binds us together and all glory
belongs to him. We can show our love and appreciation for Jesus by
how we treat other members of his body of believers.

How does your spouse fill a different role than you,
and why are you grateful for him or her?

Real Success

Keep this Book of the Law always on your lips; meditate on it day
and night, so that you may be careful to do everything written in it.
Then you will be prosperous and successful.

JOSHUA 1:8 NIV

It is commonly understood that we are what we eat—or what we
consume. When we watch too much television, we start acting like
what we view. When we listen to a lot of a certain kind of music,
it influences our behavior. When we are immersed in the Word of
God, we start behaving in accordance to what he instructed. The
only way to draw nearer to our Father is by constantly seeking his
presence, and one of the best ways to do that is by reading the Bible.

God gave us the Bible to learn who he is and what he desires. It is
a guidebook for eternal life. If your spouse gave you a book about
their life, the things they have done, and the people they have loved,
would you not pore over it? Memorize it? Surely you would take
advantage of the opportunity to know them as best as possible
because that is what you do when you love someone. Further, when
you do not understand something, you would ask them about it.
That is what God intends for us to do with his written words.

Do you struggle with meditating on the Bible?
How can you challenge each other to improve?

Price of Wisdom

The beginning of wisdom is this: Get wisdom.
Though it cost all you have, get understanding.

PROVERBS 4:7 NIV

This may seem like circular reasoning, but the insight included in these words are, in a very literal sense, soul-saving. The first step to obtaining wisdom is to recognize the value in wisdom and our need for it. This understanding and eternal perspective requires a certain amount of wisdom initially. In other words, a wise person recognizes the value in wisdom and continues to search for it at any cost.

To be wise is far greater than to be rich, successful, well connected, or even happy. Sometimes obtaining wisdom reveals injustices and other sorrowing realities, but it is still worth the price of our ignorant happiness to gain truthful understanding. Turning a blind eye to truth has the same repercussions as lying. All other opportunities, objectives, and goals should pale in comparison to our desire to receive wisdom.

What steps are you taking in your search for wisdom?

Fear God

Only fear the LORD and serve Him in truth with all your heart;
for consider what great things He has done for you.

1 SAMUEL 12:24 NASB

God is so mighty; he flooded the entire world and restarted humanity. Countless times he defeated massive armies through just a few of his faithful people. He came to earth and gave up his own rights and life so we could be made righteous. There is nothing he cannot do and no enemy he cannot defeat!

When we feel ourselves forgetting the wonders which God has done, we should read through the Old Testament and be reminded. Look at Moses in Egypt, and the lengths God went to for his people to be freed. Consider Gideon, the shy man God used to defeat the Israelites' most powerful enemy of that time. Remember David, the shepherd that God used to take down a giant. It was not his own strength that won him that victory, it was the Lord working through him. Fear of the Lord does not look like other earthly fears; it is a reverence, awe, and worship of God and his holiness.

Are you filled with the fear of the Lord?

Good Reputation

Encourage the young men to be self-controlled. In everything set them
an example by doing what is good. In your teaching show integrity,
seriousness and soundness of speech that cannot be condemned,
so that those who oppose you may be ashamed because they have
nothing bad to say about us.

TITUS 2:6-8 NIV

The way we live and the words we use should be an example to
others—especially those younger than us—of Biblical teachings
and holy living. If our teaching is pure but our actions speak
otherwise, we are hypocrites and untrustworthy. Our lifestyles
should exemplify our speech. What we say should also be carefully
examined and intentional.

Rather than being quick to offer our opinions and advice, it is
important that we exercise self-control and humility. In every area
of life, we are called to demonstrate integrity and set an example for
others. Regardless of whether other people praise our name or seek
to shame us, our intention should be to live like Jesus did and point
all honor back to him. We will not be condemned if the purpose
behind our actions and our words is to bring glory to our Father.

*When someone says something bad about you, are you quick
to defend yourself, or are you tactful, allowing your good
reputation to discredit their claims?*

Cultivating Patience

Whoever is patient has great understanding,
but one who is quick-tempered displays folly.
PROVERBS 14:29 NIV

Keeping a level head is not easy especially if we have been mistreated or antagonized. The temptation when we have been aggravated is to let loose our anger and give people our unrefined feelings. The overwhelming desire to lash out at pain and take it out on the object of our wrath is common but not condoned by God. A wise person realizes that it is God who defends us, and it is far more advantageous to show restraint, breathe, and consider the outcome of what we intend to do.

In a moment of anger and intense passion, rage overtakes reason, and the voice of the Holy Spirit is drowned out. When we fail to hear and heed the leading of the Holy Spirit, we are bound to end up sinning and going astray. This proverb serves as a warning to believers that we should not let anger and a quick temper get the best of us. It is not godly to be quick-tempered and it certainly does nothing to better the situation. Acting in self-control and maturity will bless our relationships with our spouses, friends, and the entire body of believers.

Do you have certain triggers that create angry responses?
What do these buttons reveal, and how can you bring your
responses under submission to God?

Created with Purpose

Your eyes saw my unformed body;
all the days ordained for me were written in your book
before one of them came to be.

PSALM 139:16 NIV

Each of us was created with a purpose, masterfully and in the image of God. He displays himself through his handiwork and he loves us like a perfect Father. Before we had even been formed, he already knew everything about us; how we would look, who we would love, and what our struggles and strengths would be. He ordained every day of our lives and he keeps record of us.

Any notion that Jehovah is a distant, detached God is disproved in this psalm. We all have a desire to be known and loved. Understanding someone reveals a level of closeness, the greatest of which is often shared with our spouses. The more we learn about someone we love, the dearer they become to us. There is nobody on earth who loves you the way your Creator loves you. He knows you intimately, and he is ever faithful to lead you the way you should go.

Do you make attempts to get to know your spouse better?
Do you try to get to know God better?

Delighted in You

"Before I formed you in the womb I knew you,
before you were born I set you apart;
I appointed you as a prophet to the nations."

JEREMIAH 1:4-5 NIV

Is there anything more precious than a newborn baby? They aren't delightful because they accomplished some great feat for mankind. They are precious just because they exist. As parents, godparents, or mentors, we have great aspirations for our children, and we delight to see them take those steps.

God knew us even before we were born. He delighted in us before we ever had the chance to do one good thing. He has great plans to bring him glory with our lives. How incredible to know the delight of our heavenly Father and his unique design for his children!

*Have you considered the thought that God delights in you
just because he created you?
How does this affect your thoughts toward him
and your motivation to serve him?*

New Command

> "A new commandment I give to you, that you love one another:
> just as I have loved you, you also are to love one another."
>
> JOHN 13:34 ESV

We love others not because they deserve it but because our Father loves us even when we are underserving. At times it may be difficult to find it in our hearts to extend grace, but Christ has made it possible for us through the abundant love he poured out. In fact, by forgiving us from all our wrongdoings, he has made it impossible for us to give any adequate reason why we should deny someone love.

Rarely is love earned or deserved. Love is a gift that we choose to give, sometimes when we do not want to. Often our pride threatens to get in the way, so we must intentionally lean into the grace of God and learn to love like he does. This is what makes us different and sets us apart from the rest of humanity: others will see Christ through us and know who we are by how we exhibit love.

How can you show your gratefulness to Christ
by loving your spouse even more this week?

Tuned Together

"If a house is divided against itself,
that house cannot stand."

MARK 3:25 NIV

Those who accused Jesus of being sent by Satan to do his work had no basis for their allegations. Jesus cast out demons, healed the sick, forgave sins, and did the work of the Father on earth. With this premise, he invites us into his family and his kingdom. What we must understand is that as believers, we are all one body under him. When we bicker and fight amongst each other, we cause a divide to form which threatens to topple us over. We are not unified under Christ.

Within marriage, our home is destined to fall if we cannot uphold each other and learn to submit to one another. Both partners should be in submission to God and to each other out of love, as well as to others in the faith. Our own pride and freedoms are not worth division within the church of God or our homes. Our differences should be worked through on every level in a humble and loving way which honors God.

How can you and your spouse disagree in a healthy way while maintaining unity?

Value above Worry

"Do not worry about your life, what you will eat or drink; or about your body, what you will wear. Is not life more than food, and the body more than clothes? Look at the birds of the air; they do not sow or reap or store away in barns, and yet your heavenly Father feeds them. Are you not much more valuable than they?"

MATTHEW 6:25-26 NIV

What is the motivation of your heart? As is always the case with the Jesus, he cautioned his listeners to stop worrying and keep trusting that God is good and faithful and generous. Even the birds are fed and provided for. Christ is not advocating for carelessness or irresponsibility but warning us not to obsess over money or material possessions.

Hard work is important, but our pursuit of prosperity should not be at the cost of our relationship with God, time with our family, or emotional and physical wellbeing. These are the truly valuable things in life which are worth far more than wealth. Remembering our worth and how valuable we are to God ought to remind us to recognize the various ways he cares and provides for us every single day.

Are you working in a way that is detrimental
to your relationships and health?
What can you do to ensure you keep
a healthy work life balance?

Fierce Peace

Do not be anxious about anything, but in every situation,
by prayer and petition, with thanksgiving, present your requests to God.
And the peace of God, which transcends all understanding,
will guard your hearts and your minds in Christ Jesus.

PHILIPPIANS 4:6-7 NIV

*I*t is amid travesty and despair that the peace of God really emulates from a believer's heart. When all around us is calamity, anguish, and injustice, what is within us is peace and thanksgiving. Our first response to tragedy should be prayer.

When the world reeks of anxiety and people are losing their minds, we can remember that our hearts and minds are safe because they are being guarded by the God of peace. The kind of peace he fills us with cannot be understood through human intellect; it is a peace which transcends all worldly knowledge. No matter what life may throw in our paths, our hearts and minds remain steadfast in the grace and peace of God because these gifts are of heavenly descent. God's peace is a fierce sort of peace that is stronger than anxiety or any of the cares of this world. Grab hold of it today.

How can you combat anxiety with the peace of God?
What prayers and thanksgiving can you offer to God
in difficult situations?

Be completely humble and gentle;
be patient, bearing with one another in love.
Make every effort to keep the unity of the Spirit
through the bond of peace.

EPHESIANS 4:2-3 NIV

With Integrity

The one whose walk is blameless is kept safe,
but the one whose ways are perverse will fall into the pit.
PROVERBS 28:18 NIV

Walking hand-in-hand with your spouse brings heartwarming security; walking hand-in-hand with God brings spiritual confidence. Ideally, couples join hands with each other and place their joined hands firmly in God's hand. Faith brings integrity and will keep your marriage focused on God and filled with his love.

Walking the straight and narrow path is not easy, and having a spouse to hold you accountable is a blessing. Spouses make a covenant with each other that as they walk through life they will keep each other accountable and help each other walk closely with God.

*Can you remember a time when your partner
held you accountable for an action?*

Be a Builder

Let us therefore make every effort to do
what leads to peace and to mutual edification.
ROMANS 14:19 NIV

Are our personal liberties worth causing our brothers or sisters to stumble? We are called to a higher standard: to do whatever we can to maintain peace within the family of God and to prioritize mutually edifying relationships. That does not give others the right to judge us, and we should not feel condemnation for exercising our freedoms in Christ, especially on the altar of false humility or religious appearances. But submitting our rights to the wisdom of God, not abusing our freedoms in the faces of others, and demonstrating moderation and self-control are all ways we can worship God and join him in his mission to share his love with others.

In our efforts for peace, we need to remember not to judge each other regardless of whether we agree with them or not. We are also not judged by God based on another person's feelings so, although something may be permissible, it may not always be wise.

*What is a liberty that you have which you moderate
or even abstain from for the sake of someone else?*

Strong and Courageous

"Have I not commanded you? Be strong and courageous.
Do not be afraid; do not be discouraged,
for the LORD your God will be with you wherever you go."

JOSHUA 1:9 NIV

Shortly after Moses died, the Lord spoke to Joshua and instructed him to take up the mantle and lead the people of Israel. They were to cross the Jordan River and claim the Promised Land. Regardless of the dangers or the magnitude of the task, the Lord promised Joshua that he would preserve him. Nobody could come against him and overthrow him, and everywhere he stepped would become his land. What incredible assurances to be made to one person!

Our powerful, purposeful God could do the work himself, yet he chooses to use people and reveal himself through his children. Remaining open to his leading and being courageous in our identities as his beloved and redeemed children is the best way to become involved in his plan to save the world. He eagerly uses willing individuals who chose to follow him at all costs.

How does the Word of God help you become stronger and more courageous when it comes to handling the issues of life?

Better than Fireworks

Trust in the LORD and do good.
Then you will live safely in the land and prosper.
Take delight in the LORD,
and he will give you your heart's desires.

PSALM 37:3-4 NLT

The Fourth of July is a time to celebrate America with cookouts and fireworks. It's also a good time for us to think about our blessings as a country. Sometimes we forget to thank God for his blessings of freedom—the opportunity to serve him without fear, to live safely in our country, for the opportunity to prosper, and countless other freedoms that we take for granted.

On this holiday, we can express our delight in God and thank him for his blessings—especially our freedom to worship him freely. We have a responsibility to protect that freedom for future generations, and we protect it by living in a manner where our faith impacts our culture and our homes. We can entrust our future to God, but let us work together, as husbands and wives, to keep freedom ringing throughout our land.

What freedoms are most important to you?
How can you impact this culture?

Hear and Obey

"Blessed rather are those who
hear the word of God and obey it."

LUKE 11:28 NIV

Jesus was healing the sick, teaching crowds of people, and intellectually schooling the Pharisees when a woman called out to him, "Blessed is the mother who gave you birth and nursed you" (verse 27). Jesus responded that rather than giving birth and raising the Son of God, it is even more blessed if someone were to hear the Word of God and do what it says. Obedience to the Lord is paramount in the Christian walk.

Adhering to God's statutes sets us apart from the narcissism of this world and fixes our eyes on what is eternal. All around the world, Mary, the mother of Jesus, is praised and often prayed to out of reverence for her role in God's master plan. Yet Jesus made it clear that obedience is what God honors. Mary's greatest virtue was not that she gave birth or raised a child, and it was not even her earthly parental affiliation to the Christ child. Mary was blessed by God because of her obedience to him. The same blessings are available to us.

When you read the Word of God,
do you look for ways to apply its truth to your life?

Boasting

"Those who wish to boast should boast in this alone: that they truly know me and understand that I am the LORD who demonstrates unfailing love and who brings justice and righteousness to the earth, and that I delight in these things. I, the LORD, have spoken!"

JEREMIAH 9:24 NLT

Considering the works of God's hands and the wonders he has orchestrated, boasting in our own flesh seems trite. We could feed our own egos by attempting to amaze others with our talents or accomplishments, or we could boast in the Lord by declaring his unfailing love and perfect justice for the world. He fills the earth with righteousness, and he wants to call us his friends. That is a wonder worth boasting about!

To truly know God and understand him is the greatest affiliation anyone could have. It is worth boasting in and sharing with everyone who wants to hear. Far greater it is to boast in the one who created us than to take pride in ourselves and boast in the very skills or nature that God gave us to begin with. We are on this planet for only a moment, so our sense of worth should be appropriately found in our relationship with God because only what is of him will remain.

If someone were to hear you boasting about God,
what would you be saying?

Come Boldly

Let us come boldly to the throne of our gracious God. There we will receive his mercy, and we will find grace to help us when we need it most.

HEBREWS 4:16 NLT

We do not serve a faraway god who is uncaring or aloof. The God we serve is near to anyone who calls for him, he is compassionate toward our struggles, and he extends his merciful hand to help us. He is a kind and loving Father who cares for his children. He cares so much for us that he came to earth, endured every temptation and worldly pain without sinning, and now stands as judge over the world. He knows our struggles because he experienced them too.

He invites us to come before him and ask for his help. We will receive mercy and grace from him when we ask. If earthly parents love their children enough to support them, care for them, discipline them, or even die for them, how much more does our Father in heaven love us? This sort of love did not originate with us; we are merely a reflection of God when we choose to be loving toward those around us.

When you go before God in prayer, do you feel safe to truly open your heart and ask him for mercy?

Eternal Contentment

Make sure that your character is free from the love of money,
being content with what you have; for He Himself has said,
"I will never desert you, nor will I ever forsake you."

HEBREWS 13:5 NASB

Those who are led around by a love for money will never know contentment in Christ. They will be easily led and manipulated because money is fickle and easy to lose. Security cannot be found in money; it can only be found in God who faithfully promises to never forsake us. Wealth can give no such assurance. Proper use of money can be a blessing, since money itself is not evil. When greed flares up, money can become a stronghold in someone's heart and push aside the love of God.

God is not willing to share his lordship with anyone or anything else because he alone is worthy. Therefore, we cannot submit ourselves both to him and to the pursuit of money. If we make lots of money in our obedience to God and in using the gifts which he has given us, then let us use that money to praise him and love others. If we make barely enough to get by, let us continue to praise him and find everlasting contentment in his grace.

How do you and your spouse ensure that your pursuit hasn't shifted away from God and toward making money?

Getting Advice

Get all the advice and instruction you can,
so you will be wise the rest of your life.

PROVERBS 19:20 NLT

Life gets the best of us all at times, and we are left wondering what to do in particular situations. It may be that we have never faced certain situations before, or that we simply have not practiced wisdom in some of the choices we made. There is an African saying which teaches that an old man can see sitting down what a young man cannot see while standing in a tree. In other words, it is a good idea to heed wise advice, especially from a trusted source that has time and experience on their side.

Self-discipline is vital if we intend to accomplish anything worthwhile. Even the most menial tasks require discipline to undertake. It is good practice to listen to advice and accept correction, since this approach with God is how we attain wisdom. Discipline and wisdom go together; in fact, an undisciplined person cannot find wisdom since it is hidden with Christ. By applying simple, fundamental lessons from God's Word to our lives, we grow in wisdom and understanding. God's Word is not only a lamp to our feet and a light to our path, it is life itself.

Who do you and your spouse ask for advice?

Give Generously

They share freely and give generously to those in need.
Their good deeds will be remembered forever.
They will have influence and honor.

PSALM 112:9 NLT

The things which God delights in and the things the world delights in are very different. It is better to be on the side of delighting God since his opinion is the one that matters. The world will love us and then it will hate us. We cannot rely on the world to sustain us. On the other hand, God can bestow honor and dishonor, he can sustain us for all of eternity, and his love is unbreakable.

The works of the righteous are pleasing to God, and he gives them both influence and honor. Righteous people live to love and serve since they are made in the image of God. They are not easily frightened nor become worried when receiving bad news because their hearts are steadfast in God. Their enemies have no power over them because they look to their Maker for protection. From what they have, they give what they can in order to help those in need. Even their giving is joyful and wrought in gratitude. It is acts like this which will be forever remembered.

How can you and your spouse live righteously together?

For You

What shall we say about such wonderful things as these? If God is for us, who can ever be against us? Since he did not spare even his own Son but gave him up for us all, won't he also give us everything else?

ROMANS 8:31-32 NLT

God is for you. He's on your side. How can you be sure? According to Romans 6, the cross is proof. God did not spare his own Son but gave him up for you, so that you could be fully forgiven and adopted into his family. He helps you in your weaknesses. The Holy Spirit prays for you according to God's own will. God causes everything to work out for good and he has chosen you! Nothing can separate you from his love.

In light of that, does it really matter if others oppose you, or if you make a terrible choice? Consequences will come, but God is still on your side. He's waiting to mend the rips and forgive your sin. If you have Jesus, you have everything!

Do you need to be reminded today that God is on your side?
Are you on each other's sides,
supporting and cheering each other on?

Growing Up

Anyone who lives on milk, being still an infant, is not acquainted with the teaching about righteousness. But solid food is for the mature, who by constant use have trained themselves to distinguish good from evil.

HEBREWS 5:14 NIV

There's nothing wrong with being a babe in Christ. Everyone begins at the beginning. However, when one remains in the infant stage, or digresses back to it because of malnourishment, there is a problem. Paul was frustrated by the lack of understanding as he taught on the meatier subjects of faith. He said they were dull of hearing. Their spiritual immaturity was apparent. For the amount of time they had followed Jesus, they should have been teachers rather than elementary school kids.

It's good to evaluate our spiritual growth, remembering that it is our responsibility. We grow in spiritual maturity by dining on the solid food of the Word and trusting God to teach us through it. We can't wait around for someone else to make sure we grow up in God.

As a couple, are you complacent or disinterested
in going deeper with God?
Are you more enamored with things in this world
than you are with seeking things above?

Humble Harmony

Never pay back evil with more evil.
Do things in such a way that everyone can see you are honorable.
ROMANS 12:17 NLT

We cannot control the decisions of other people and we cannot always control what happens to us. What we do have power over is our response. Another person's sin does not permit us to retaliate with more sin. We have the option in those moments to either sink to the level of the perpetrator, or to become more like Christ.

In order to practice forgiveness, we first need someone to forgive. Anyone can love someone who is loveable but choosing to love someone who intended harm toward us displays the love of Christ. Rather than become defensive and strike back, we should view these times as opportunities to live as Christ. It requires humility to live in harmony with others, but when we have the mind of Christ it is far more conceivable. Christ did not pay our evil back with evil, but instead covered it with love. Love is more powerful than hate because love can reach places that hate cannot.

*What happens when you respond
with love toward your spouse?*

Iron Bars

*A brother who has been insulted is harder to win back than a walled city,
and arguments separate people like the barred gates of a palace.*
PROVERBS 18:19 NCV

*O*ur verse today paints a vivid picture of what can happen when a disagreement between family members becomes an offense. Iron bars of resentment are almost impossible to remove. Small matters mushroom into deep, irreparable rifts between those we once loved and trusted. For all our love, there is often less mercy for those we are closest to than to mere acquaintances or strangers.

Consider offences between brothers in Scripture. Cain killed Abel out of jealousy. Esau sought to kill Jacob for stealing away his blessing. Joseph's envious brothers sold him into slavery. Even Paul and Barnabas had a sharp disagreement about taking Mark with them on a missionary journey. Mending these kinds of broken relationships is as difficult as conquering a fortified city. Here is the lesson: Guard your marriage carefully. Avoid conflict and contention, and when it happens, reconcile quickly. Don't let resentments brew.

*Are you stewing over some disagreement
that you have not brought to light?
If so, talk about it, and make things right.*

Be Still

> "Be still, and know that I am God.
> I will be exalted among the nations,
> I will be exalted in the earth!"
>
> PSALM 46:10 ESV

The lyrics of this mighty song were written to the Sons of Korah and historians believe it was during a time of strife or war in Israel. The whole psalm is written in third person until verse ten when, as we see, it shifts to second person. Instead of the psalmist proclaiming encouragement and the wonderful attributes of the Lord, Yahweh is now speaking directly to the people of Israel and declaring who he is.

Stop striving. You do not fight alone. Turn to the one who is exalted to farthest reaches of the earth and watch him work his wonders! Be still before him and take time to heed the voice of your Maker. It is he alone who every nation will praise, and who the entirety of humanity will bow before. When we face trials, rather than brazenly pushing forward or cowering in dismay, we need to intentionally be still before God so we can witness his power and learn how we ought to walk.

Have you taken time to be still before God today?
What battles are you facing that need to be submitted to him?

Unquenchable Love

Many waters cannot quench love;
rivers cannot sweep it away.
If one were to give all the wealth of one's house for love,
it would be utterly scorned.

SONG OF SOLOMON 8:7 NIV

Who would not desire to have the undying love described in the beautiful account of the Song of Solomon? Here we see a young woman in love with a poor shepherd boy. They both know they will not have much material wealth in life, but they have grown to love each other so ardently that even though the young woman was offered all the riches and comforts of the wealthiest man on earth in exchange for her hand in marriage, she refused to even consider it. In the verse preceding this one, she tells Solomon that the fire of love is as the fire of Jehovah, which is why it is unquenchable!

While most would not think of trading true love for material things, we sometimes put ourselves in a position of working so much to gain wealth or prestige that we actually neglect our marriage. While we should be good workers, we also must be content with what we have and put more value on our marriage. If the intense love described in the Song of Solomon has burned low in your heart, work hard together to rekindle the flame so that even a river cannot extinguish it!

*What material things have held greater appeal
than your love for your spouse?
How can you change your heart?*

Love that Lasts

Always be humble and gentle. Be patient with each other,
making allowance for each other's faults because of your love.
EPHESIANS 4:2 NCV

Paul is not saying that we should tolerate sin, since sin is abhorrent to God. He is addressing the way we approach someone who is sinning. Oftentimes sin is a symptom of a deeper underlying issue. They may feel insecure or unloved, or they may have believed a lie. Whatever the case is, aggressively disputing their sin or their fault will only heighten the problem they are already facing.

If we lord our "righteousness" over others in an attempt to convict them of their sin, they may shirk back or become defensive. We must be humble and remember everything we have been forgiven of. Gentleness creates a safe environment for people to share their troubles. Patience is important because rarely is change immediate. Most of all, love is vital because it is what binds us together.

When your spouse is at fault,
do you hold it over them,
or do you gently forgive them?

Loving the World

> Do not love the world or the things in the world. If anyone loves the world, the love of the Father is not in him. For all that is in the world—the desires of the flesh and the desires of the eyes and pride of life are not from the Father but are from the world.
>
> 1 JOHN 2:15-16 ESV

Someone who does not love the things of this world cannot be controlled by the powers of this world. When our love is for our Father, we will be led safely by our Father. We cannot live in two kingdoms. We were placed in this world and it is not wrong to live to the fullest measure here and now, but we need to maintain an eternal perspective that reminds us of where we are going.

The three types of desires John addresses here—the desires of the flesh, the desires of the eyes, and the pride of life—are not referring to natural, human desires but when they encompass more of our heart than God does. For instance, being led around by what our flesh wants, or our eyes see rather than what God wants is putting our love and allegiance into the world, not our Lord. When we starve the pride of life, we are choosing to love and serve God rather than ourselves.

What are some examples of the three worldly desires that could draw your focus away from God?

Needing Help

> Where there is no guidance the people fall,
> but in abundance of counselors there is victory.
>
> PROVERBS 11:14 NASB

Solomon, the wisest man who ever lived, still needed help, and he didn't allow his pride to stand in the way. When Solomon built the temple, he needed more talent and supplies than Israel could provide, including skilled carpenters, stonecutters, and a great amount of cedar wood. He enlisted the help of King Hiram, and after seven and a half years, the completed project was one of the wonders of the world.

It takes humility to ask for help. Many marriages do not endure because the couple is simply not willing to admit to anyone that they need advice. Pride can stand in the way of tapping into the resources of wisdom that God has placed in others.

Do you need help with your marriage,
your finances, or your parenting?
Assess your needs and talk about
who you can get support and godly advice from.
Don't let pride stand in your way.

Healthy Ways

No discipline seems pleasant at the time, but painful.
Later on, however, it produces a harvest of righteousness and peace
for those who have been trained by it.

HEBREWS 12:11 NIV

Caring parents teach their children right from wrong. They guide them in healthy, safe ways, and discipline them when they misbehave. Understanding cause and effect is necessary for a child to learn how to take care of themselves and navigate through life. If actions do not lead to reactions—good and bad—then we are free to do whatever we please regardless of the outcome.

It is only through consequences that we learn how to make good decisions. We do not like discipline, but it is a loving lesson from our Father because he wants us to mature and do well. It is a sure sign that the Lord is working in our lives. If we are wise enough to heed his interjection and learn from it, we will become more righteous and find peace. Training requires discipline to follow through, humility to learn, and determination to keep going. The Lord's training should not dishearten us but encourage us that growth is happening.

How do you sense the Lord guiding you in healthy, safe ways?

Our Safe Place

The LORD is a refuge for the oppressed,
a stronghold in times of trouble.
PSALM 9:9 NIV

Trouble is guaranteed for those who live according to the Word of God. This world and its systems are not designed after Biblical principles, and we who live righteously cannot conform to the patterns established throughout our society. There are times when we need deliverance, either from oppression or temptation. When those times come, it is the Lord who we must turn to. No amount of personal strength can carry us farther than the cross is able. Our safe place, our refuge from trouble, is found in God. He promises to be our stronghold, and his arms are open wide for his children.

There is no power on this earth that can destroy a Christian when they have sought the protection of God. David knew this even in the midst of war, personal temptation, and betrayal. His hope was secure as was his faith. Plant yourself firmly in the only one who can deliver you from every attack of the enemy and every single one of your personal sins.

Have you sought God with your spouse and asked him
to surround your marriage, so it may be an extension
of his refuge, a safe place free from oppression?

Mouths of Babes

He called a child, whom he put among them, and said,
"Truly I tell you, unless you change and become like children,
you will never enter the kingdom of heaven."

MATTHEW 18:2-3 NRSV

Jesus' disciples asked him who the greatest in the kingdom of heaven was. There had been bickering among them and pride was beginning to fester in their hearts. We all want to feel important, but our importance comes from our identity in Christ, not from our stature or position. Jesus clarified this perfectly when he motioned to a child and announced that they needed to become like a child in order to enter the kingdom of heaven.

Christ's followers were constantly trying to appear knowledgeable and important in the eyes of each other. Children are not distinguished, respected leaders of society. Children are obedient, dependent, and innocent of a lot of things. They are led by others, and they have a sort of humility that grows thin as they age. In order to enter the kingdom of heaven, Jesus tells us to revert to when we were dependent, humble, and childlike. That is his definition of greatness in his perfectly paradoxical kingdom.

What does it mean to have childlike faith?

Bitter Roots

Look after each other so that none of you fails to receive the grace of God.
Watch out that no poisonous root of bitterness grows up to trouble you,
corrupting many.

HEBREWS 12:15 NLT

What we see is often determined by the unseen. While we see only a plant's stem and leaves, hidden underground is a complex, life-giving root system. The roots are anchors for the plant; they take up water and nutrients from the soil and propel them to the stems and leaves. Healthy roots make a healthy plant and produce good fruit.

In the Hebrew culture, a poisonous plant was called a bitter plant. The writer of Hebrews uses this metaphor to warn the church against the poison of bitterness in the heart. Hatred, hostility, cynicism, resentment, and anger can become flourishing root systems in the heart that feed the spirit with bitterness and poison others. We must watch carefully for poisonous roots. Bitter roots produce bitter fruit.

Have you allowed bitterness to take root in your heart?
Is there anyone you need to forgive or an offense
that you need to release to God?
Are you upset with one another?
Talk about all of these bitter roots.

Unwholesome Talk

Do not let any unwholesome talk come out of your mouths,
but only what is helpful for building others up according to their needs,
that it may benefit those who listen.

EPHESIANS 4:29 NIV

*O*ur words carry power. We can use them to build up or break down, to spread truth or lies, to praise God or bring shame on ourselves. We are also responsible for our words on social media. It might be more tempting to use cruel or vulgar language when looking at a screen instead of another person's face, but the impact is the same. The words are still intended for and heard by other people.

James likened our tongues to a fire which has the power to spread and destroy. In one moment, we may be speaking blessings and praising God, but the next we are tearing someone down or gossiping about them. Since all humans are God's beloved creations, we are disgracing his handiwork when we participate in such foolish talk. James even said that blessing and cursing cannot come from the same heart any more than fresh water and salty water can flow from the same spring. Our words reveal the condition of our hearts, so let's ensure our hearts are full of love and grace.

When you are tempted to use unwholesome talk,
what can you do instead?

Shine Like Stars

Do all things without murmuring and arguing, so that you may be
blameless and innocent, children of God without blemish in the midst of a
crooked and perverse generation, in which you shine like stars in the world.
PHILIPPIANS 2:14-15 NRSV

*D*o you want to be blameless and innocent, a beacon for Jesus in
our dark world? Then learn a lesson from the Israelites. Three days
out from God's mighty, miraculous deliverance from Pharaoh, they
began the persistent, besetting sin of complaining. There was no
fresh water; there was no food; there was no meat. God met their
needs faithfully, but they were never satisfied for long. It was a bad
testimony to the nations around them.

Complaining and arguing about our circumstances, about each
other, or about our lot in life is insulting to our Savior. It says to
him that what he has provided isn't good enough. For the sake of
honoring Christ and providing a good example to others, let us do
everything without murmuring!

Are you a complainer?
Do you naturally default to the negative
and voice your displeasure?
Talk about how you can share positivity
and hold each other accountable.

Following

You shall follow the LORD your God and fear Him;
and you shall keep His commandments,
listen to His voice, serve Him, and cling to Him.
DEUTERONOMY 13:4 NASB

*O*ften the Bible contrasts good with evil, obedience with rebellion, and so forth. It will detail the destruction of the wicked and then reveal the rewards of the righteous. Here, the Scriptures warn about false prophets, especially when their predictions come true. If they attempt to lead us to worship other gods, we are to refuse.

What is the best way to refuse? This verse, immediately following the warning, outlines it perfectly. Each of these six directives—follow, fear, obey, listen, serve, and cling—will give us the resistance we need to see through the lies and avoid the snares. We will not become manipulated by the devil's tricks when we know the truth. God is the actual miracle worker and Savior of mankind, everything else is only a copy of the original. Spending time with him familiarizes us with the sound of his voice. Clinging to him keeps us from falling. He will keep us from going astray.

Do you ever worry about being tricked?
How can you better familiarize yourself
with God's truth together so you can identify lies?

With God

In keeping with his promise we are looking forward to a new heaven
and a new earth, where righteousness dwells.

2 PETER 3:13 NIV

Whether Peter is inferring that a new heaven and earth will be
created, or whether God intends to purify the current ones and
make them like new has been a debated issue for hundreds of years.
It is difficult to surmise the complete intent of this verse; however,
the important part is that we will be where righteousness dwells.
Since God is righteousness, we understand that this means we will
be with God. What is more incredible than that?

Peter's words align with Paul's revelation of the end of days when he
said, "God himself will be with them as their God" (Revelation 21:1).
Regardless of how it unfolds, our greatest hope and most astounding
promise is that one day we will live with God! Believing this offers us
great endurance in this life because, as unjust and unloving as love
can be at times, that will all one day pass away, and we will be left in
the presence of the one who is perfect.

*What creation in nature inspires your imagination
and makes you wonder about the new heaven and earth?*

Freedom of Forgiveness

"Lord, how often shall my brother sin against me and I forgive him?
Up to seven times?"
Jesus said to him, "I do not say to you, up to seven times,
but up to seventy times seven."
MATTHEW 18:21-22 NASB

The instructions Jesus gave to Peter regarding forgiveness both superseded Jewish tradition and held a deeper association with a well-known Old Testament passage. It was custom among the Jews to offer forgiveness up to three times. Peter, believing he was being more than generous, asked his Rabbi if seven times would suffice.

In essence, Jesus was saying that forgiveness should be limitless, just like God's forgiveness toward us. A long time before this conversation transpired, the young earth saw two murders: Cain and Lamech. Since God had already issued discipline to Cain, nobody was allowed to hurt him further. The punishment issued would be sevenfold. Lamech then announced that the retribution for harming him would be seventy times seven (Genesis 4:24). This testimony of violence and vengeance would have been well-known to Peter and the Jews. Jesus wisely used it to illustrate the power of forgiveness, which is far stronger and lasting than revenge.

*Can you show forgiveness to your spouse as many times
as needed without seeking reciprocity or reward?*

Great Exchange

You know the generous grace of our Lord Jesus Christ.
Though he was rich, yet for your sakes he became poor,
so that by his poverty he could make you rich.

2 CORINTHIANS 8:9 NLT

History books are full of accounts of great men and women who sacrificed for the sake of others. However, there has never been a story that comes close to what Christ did for us. Yes, people have died cruel, undeserving deaths, but only Christ took the world's weight of sin on himself and carried it to the grave for us.

How can one follow Christ in this? Is it possible to make the greatest of all exchanges, one for another? At the cost of his life, Christ lavished his kindness, gracious generosity, and undeserved favor on us. How can we possibly emulate him? Perhaps we can in small, everyday ways. We can put our own desires on the shelf to prefer another's. We can consider others' needs above our own. We can drop our agenda and pick up someone else's. In all these ways, we put others first and love them sacrificially.

Take a few moments to apply these general statements
to your relationship as husband and wife.
Do you set aside your own desires and serve each other?

Habit of Prayer

Very early in the morning, while it was still dark, Jesus got up,
left the house and went off to a solitary place, where he prayed.

MARK 1:35 NIV

The day before had been a full one for Jesus. He had spent the whole day in Capernaum healing the sick and attending to as many people as came to him. The busy day did not hinder Jesus from rising early the following morning to spend time in prayer. More important than sleep or any other human need is our relationship with the Father, and Jesus was demonstrating that for us.

When we feel overwhelmed and overworked, it is important to stay connected to God. He is our source of strength and encouragement. Fostering a habit of prayer will help us stay on course and not drift. It will keep us aligned with God's will and plan. Prayer is essential for our well-being and Jesus knew that. When we are not listening to God's voice, we are susceptible to other voices who may try to mislead us. In marriage, we have someone else who can remind us and encourage us to pray, and they can also pray for us. What a blessing that can be.

Do you have a habit of prayer in your life?
If not, what can you do to create one?

The Listening Ear

You must all be quick to listen,
slow to speak,
and slow to get angry.

JAMES 1:19 NLT

There is nothing more frustrating than trying to communicate something important to an inattentive listener. Checking a phone, over-the-shoulder glances, and restless hands are sure signs that your words are ricocheting around in space and not making a connection. Good listeners are not waiting for a slight lull to begin their own monologue. They keep eye contact, act interested, and respond appropriately.

James speaks extensively in his book about the power and destructiveness of the tongue. Here, his first command for the tongue is to silence it! Instead of talking, listen. Slow down and listen without jumping to conclusions.

Do you listen to one another?
Do you give each other your full attention
in order to understand?
Do you easily jump to conclusions or rush to judgment?
Talk with your spouse about where listening is good
and where it can improve.

Place me like a seal over your heart,
like a seal on your arm.
For love is as strong as death,
its jealousy as enduring as the grave.

SONG OF SOLOMON 8:6 NLT

Trained for Battle

God arms me with strength, and he makes my way perfect.
He makes me as surefooted as a deer,
enabling me to stand on mountain heights.
He trains my hands for battle;
he strengthens my arm to draw a bronze bow.

PSALM 18:32-34 NLT

You and your spouse are a team. Together you have a collection of skills, talents, and passions that make your team unique. You can't compare your relationship to others in all respects because there is no other couple exactly like you. As soon as you said, "I do," the two of you began to form habits, rituals, and routines. You took on certain jobs.

As time goes by and the dynamics of married life change, you need to find ways to be flexible. All days are not the same; all seasons in your lives will not go exactly as you plan. God has prepared you with tools and savvy to use the intelligence and competence you both possess to aid you in all circumstances. When you encounter bumps in the road, seek guidance and help from the Lord. All you are and all you have comes from him. Trust him to continue to supply your needs as you walk forward.

Do you have a hard time accepting change, or are you flexible?
What talent or skill do you possess
that will help your relationship in the future?
Why do you think change elicits a certain response in you?

Do Good

Let us think of ways to motivate one another
to acts of love and good works.
HEBREWS 10:24 NLT

God's beautiful design for the body of Christ was that we should live together in unity, help each other through difficulties, and encourage one another toward love and good works. It is not God's intention that we isolate and attempt to walk out our faith alone. We are motivated by the words—sometimes just the presence—of others. When difficult times come, rather than draw inward and cut off from other people, we should look for ways to motivate others and inspire them to keep pressing toward love and good works.

If we ourselves are feeling unmotivated or unloved, the temptation is often to distance ourselves and detach from others, but that is not how the Bible teaches us to cope. Instead of numbing our minds through media and entertainment, we should find someone else to interact with who can encourage us to keep going. Maybe your spouse is that someone else.

What motivates you to keep going?
How do you like to motivate others?

Ask for Directions

Look here, you who say, "Today or tomorrow we are going to a certain town and will stay there a year. We will do business there and make a profit." How do you know what your life will be like tomorrow? Your life is like the morning fog—it's here a little while, then it's gone. What you ought to say is, "If the Lord wants us to, we will live and do this or that."

JAMES 4:13-15 NLT

There are moments in life when we realize how little control we have over our own fate. There are people and powers far stronger than us in this world, and often we are at the mercy of their decisions. Plans are created and cancelled regularly, and we must constantly be adapting to whatever the day holds. Disappointment is common, and still we must make plans.

It would be foolish to not have plans for our lives, yet James is explaining that our intentions should never supersede God's directions. Instead of obstinately insisting on sticking to the plan, our hearts should be open to hear what God is saying and recognize where he is leading. It is enough that we know God and his trustworthy reputation; we can fully rely on him to lead us tomorrow as well.

What plans do you have for your life?
Are you constantly submitting them to God?

Gracious Holmes

The Word became flesh, and dwelt among us, and we saw His glory,
glory as of the only begotten from the Father, full of grace and truth.
JOHN 1:14 NASB

The Word of God is an actual picture of Jesus. All through the Old Testament are signs of the coming Messiah. Once Jesus arrived and dwelled among his people, the gospels testified of it. Following the gospels, the rest of the New Testament declares Christ's goodness and how we ought to follow him.

The entirety of the Holy Scriptures is the testimony of Jesus Christ. He is the Word of God. He came literally in the flesh as a man so that he would experience every hardship and temptation that his people do and walk through them sinless to show us the way. He was and is the glory of God because he is God! The term John used to describe him here as "begotten from the Father" is the same one he used later in the well-known verse John 3:16. The term is *monogenes* which means Jesus is the one and only God.

Why would the Almighty God of heaven
come and dwell among his people?

Nazarene Neighbors

Jesus traveled to Nazareth, where he had grown up. On the Sabbath day he
went to the synagogue, as he always did, and stood up to read.

LUKE 4:16 NCV

Jesus had recently concluded his forty day fast in the desert where
he was tempted by the devil. Having overcome, he returned to
Galilee and went to Nazareth. Taking a scroll which had the words
of the prophet Isaiah inscribed on it, he stood before the familiar
faces of his hometown. Then he read, "The Spirit of the Lord is
upon me, because he has anointed me to proclaim good news to the
poor.…" When he finished, he told them that today this prophesy
was fulfilled.

Everyone in the synagogue was transfixed by him. They knew he
was Joseph's son, yet was he claiming to be God. Jesus continued to
speak, but they were furious and attempted to kill him. Sometimes
it is most difficult to bring up controversial truths with those who
know us best, and yet truth must always be on our lips. Jesus knew
he would be rejected, but because of his love for his people, he
continued to teach the good news of God's salvation plan.

*Are you willing to share the truth of the gospel
with those closest to you?*

Keep the Peace

"Every kingdom divided against itself will be ruined,
and every city or household divided against itself will not stand."
MATTHEW 12:25 NIV

*D*ivisions can start off small. They might be a few different thoughts with the way a friend is doing things, or it may come out in a few disgruntled comments to your co-workers. Chances are you have made it clear to your spouse when they have irritated you.

If there are children in your household, there are more opportunities for disharmony, between siblings or your parenting styles. We need to actively look for common ground and keep God's will for our families at the forefront. Be encouraged that God didn't make us exactly the same; he made us to complement one another.

*Are you letting your spouse or your kids
bring out the best in you?
Think of the areas that need some adjusting
and bring them to the Holy Spirit in prayer.*

Practice Love

Dear children, let us not love with words or speech
but with actions and in truth.
1 JOHN 3:18 NIV

Professing love is important, but it is proven through our actions. If our words do not match our deeds, what weight do our words truly hold? Jesus came preaching love, but he also showed it through the way he lived. He washed his disciples' feet, he healed the sick and raised the dead, he wept with those who mourned, he lived a modest life, and he withstood ridicule and false accusations. Finally, in a true test of love, he endured a horrific death to free us from the bondages of sin.

Jesus' love was evident to all in the way he lived his life. Simply saying we love someone is not the same as showing them. Marriage is the perfect place to practice love. Wedded union is not a mutual agreement that all should be fair and both parties do their part. The love that Jesus showed us, his bride, was not even close to fair. Marriage is a commitment to love and serve each other even when it is not fair. Love cares about the other person even unto death.

Have you told your spouse that you love them today?
Do your actions prove it?

Humble Arguments

When pride comes, then comes disgrace,
but with humility comes wisdom.
PROVERBS 11:2 NIV

Pride often pushes us to show off what we know, and sometimes it leads us to say foolish things that we have not thought through. If we are wrong, or if it was inappropriately said, we bring disgrace on ourselves. Our own proud words and focusing on making ourselves sound important bring us shame.

A humble heart will first listen to others. It considers whether what it wants to say is beneficial and godly or self-serving and foolish before speaking. It uses wisdom to direct its speech in a way that brings glory to God rather than attention to itself. In keeping with this standard, we can argue with others in a humble and impactful way. We do not have to agree with what other people say, but we do need to treat them with respect since they are also created in the image of God and are dearly loved by him.

*When your spouse questions your words or decisions,
how can you respond in a way that is respectful and honoring
both to them and to God?*

Surviving the Drought

Though the fig tree does not bud and there are no grapes on the vines,
though the olive crop fails and the fields produce no food, though there are
no sheep in the pen and no cattle in the stalls, yet I will rejoice in the LORD,
I will be joyful in God my Savior.

HABAKKUK 3:17-18 NIV

Droughts are a real and natural part of any lasting relationship. We can find ourselves facing seasons of life that seem unproductive, discouraging, and just plain dry. In these times, your love might feel dormant.

If you are experiencing this right now, be encouraged to find the depth of character that comes with persevering through droughts. If you both agree to face dry times together, you will find that your love will come into a new season. Praise God and find his joy in every circumstance.

*Are you experiencing a dry season in your relationship?
Do you feel there is no fruit in your lives?
Take some time to consider what season of life you are in,
and plan for future droughts.*

Considered Conversations

These commandments that I give you today are to be on your hearts.
Impress them on your children. Talk about them when you sit at home and
when you walk along the road, when you lie down and when you get up.

DEUTERONOMY 6:6-7 NIV

What dominates conversations between you and your spouse? Is it the next purchase, holiday, or chore? Is it your work or your children? Perhaps you spend a lot of time discussing finances or people you know. It's okay to talk about what is on your mind, but do you give much thought to the Scriptures and how God might be speaking to you throughout your day?

If you have children, chances are they are going to pick up on a lot of your dialogue. When the Word of God is on our hearts, we naturally spend time talking about Jesus at home, when we're out, and as we go to bed. Pass your love for God's ways on. Discuss them with your family. When you share your heart, others will be able to share theirs.

What have you spent a lot of time talking about recently?
Can you think of ways to bring Jesus
into your conversations with each other?

Nearsighted

"How can you think of saying, 'Friend, let me help you get rid of that speck in your eye,' when you can't see past the log in your own eye?"

LUKE 6:42 NLT

As humans, we are so hasty to find fault in others, forgetting quickly to handle our own affairs. Sin truly does blind us, and it can become a tendency to want to find fault in others to normalize the sin we are guilty of ourselves. In truth, this sort of spiritual nearsightedness not only stunts our growth but renders us incapable to help others. How can we possibly see clearly enough to assist others in overcoming their issues if we have not dealt with the sin in our own lives?

A humble and contrite heart is imperative for growing in godliness and being used by God to help others as well. Luke made it clear that we will receive in like measure what we offer to others. If we judge, we will be judged. If we condemn, we will be condemned. However, if we forgive, we will be forgiven. If we give to others, God will give us more than we can imagine! He is a fair and generous God.

What do you need to work on in your own heart?

Received

"Anyone who receives you receives me,
and anyone who receives me receives the Father who sent me."
MATTHEW 10:40 NLT

People marry with the best intentions not to make the same mistakes their parents did. Then, reality hits. The wife finds herself getting irritated when her husband doesn't pick up his clothes and leaves shaved facial hairs in the sink, and the husband gets upset because his wife is picky and hard to please. When they are calm and not in a pointing-fingers mood, loving spouses will hear each other out and humbly ask for forgiveness, promising change. What if that only works for a week?

The verse for today compels us to look beyond ourselves and our problems. Jesus says to receive our spouses as if we were receiving him. Wow! In other words, look beyond your spouse's shortcomings, and receive him or her as you do Christ.

How can we acknowledge Christ's presence each morning
as we start our day and look beyond each other's faults?

Creator and Judge

Who are you, O man, to answer back to God?
Will what is molded say to its molder,
"Why have you made me like this?"
ROMANS 9:20 ESV

A popular belief dished out to today's young people is that they can be anything they aspire to be. The big flaw in this encouragement is the assessment of ability. You always benefit from hard work and practice, but what if your gifts don't line up with your desires? At times, we all fall prey to longing for different talents.

We are content when we accept our gifts, and we must accept our spouse's gifts as well. So your husband isn't a handyman, but perhaps he quickly spots the flaws in a theological argument. Maybe your wife doesn't feel comfortable in the kitchen, but she loves to paint and creates beautiful art. Rejoice with and encourage your spouse to excel in his or her gifts.

How can you accept the unique gifts
God gave you and your spouse?
Brainstorm ways you can use those gifts in the coming weeks.

Bonds of Peace

Make every effort to keep yourselves united in the Spirit,
binding yourselves together with peace.
EPHESIANS 4:3 NLT

Christ did not call us to a life of tolerance of other Christians or of apathy toward them. He does not even expect us to keep distance from each other in order to avoid conflict. His intention for his children is that we fight for each other and fellowship together. We are to make every effort for unity with our brothers and sisters in Christ. Paul even goes so far as to use the analogy of "bonds," of which he was no stranger. He had himself been bound together with other prisoners in jail and knew what it was like to be shackled with nowhere to hide.

There are some days when marriage is not easy, and rather than avoid the issues, we are instructed to put forth every effort to work through them for the sake of our unity. Some days may even feel like we are shackled in jail together, but peace and love are so important that we ought to praise God for our shackles and thank him for each other.

What sort of efforts can you make
to pursue peace and unity in your marriage?

Sharing Wisdom

Wise people can also listen and learn;
even they can find good advice in these words.

PROVERBS 1:5 NCV

The stats prove what we all suspected: in general, women talk more than men. The numbers vary from 15,000 words a day to 30,000, but the average woman speaks three times more than the average man. Have you observed couples walking—be it on a street, path, or beach—and often the woman is talking, while the man listens? The need to talk is part of a woman's DNA, and that hasn't changed since the beginning of time.

When a wife comes to her husband with a question, she isn't always looking for a solution. She just needs to talk it out, and in talking, she often finds the answer. If a husband doesn't know that, he gets out his mental tool box to suggest a fix. The wise wife will preface her talk by saying, "I'm not looking for solutions. I just need to dump on someone." The wise husband will then listen attentively, without offering solutions or three steps to solving her problems.

How can you improve your dialogue?
Talk together about communicating clearly.

Understanding

As you do not know the path of the wind,
or how the body is formed in a mother's womb,
so you cannot understand the work of God,
the Maker of all things.

ECCLESIASTES 11:5 NIV

The only thing certain in this world is that things are uncertain. We can predict the weather, but only God knows the path of the wind. Plans can be formed, but in an instant they can change. The Lord creates life. We have power over neither life nor death. We can make plans, but only God knows how to form the perfect body of a baby within a woman. All things are in his hands. If we plan our lives according to our own desires and intents, we will face many disappointments and frustrations.

The Maker of heaven and earth, the one who creates life, he who directs the wind, the King who all of nature submits to is the only certain hope that we have. If we place our plans in his hands and we live according to his desires, we will always have surety that everything will work out well in the end.

What do you do when your plans are disappointed?
Do you try to control the situation,
or do you go back to God for directions?

Cause and Effect

A glad heart makes a cheerful face,
but by sorrow of heart the spirit is crushed.
PROVERBS 15:13 ESV

The condition of our hearts has an effect on our physical demeanor. A smile adds a lot more to a lady's countenance than makeup ever could, and a man who is joyful is so much more pleasurable to be around than a despondent one regardless of his physique. Joy and sorrow are much deeper than happiness and sadness. Circumstances can affect our moods, but we cannot allow them to change the condition of our hearts. Our hearts beat for our Savior, and we are joyful because of what he has done for us!

Even when tragedy hits and we are grieving, we can still cling to joy because of the hope and the love Jesus has filled us with. He gives us a peace that goes beyond human understanding and is stronger than any situation we may experience. When we have this joy in our hearts, it radiates through our being. Others will notice it and may even be encouraged by it. The masterful cause and effect of following the Lord is immediate, powerful, and contagious.

*How can the joy you experience and carry in your heart
be a blessing to your spouse as well?*

Praise Wins

Through the praise of children and infants
you have established a stronghold against your enemies,
to silence the foe and the avenger.

PSALM 8:2 NIV

Whenever God chooses to use the weak things of this world rather than what we see as strong, he proves that true strength comes only from him. When the daughter of Pharaoh found Baby Moses crying in the reeds, her heart was moved for him. By that baby's cry, a chain of events was set in motion that would one day take down the entire Egyptian army. When Christ came as a baby into this world, he terrified the powers of earth through Herod as well as the armies of Hades! They knew their days of reigning and oppressing we numbered.

Praising God goes a long way toward actual change and the conditions of our hearts. Sometimes as adults we overcomplicate things or try to control more than we should. Children are used to not having much control over their lives. They are still naïve. Their praises carry great power because their innocent dependence on God and appreciation of him is pleasing to him.

When was the last time you released control to God
and simply praised him for his goodness?

Set in Stone

You can make many plans,
but the LORD's purpose will prevail.
PROVERBS 19:21 NLT

The obvious separation of wisdom and understanding between the mind of the Lord and that of a mortal human should be convicting enough that it is by God's divine intent only that we live and act and have meaning. Spiritual truths beyond our comprehension dictate where our paths lead. Even understanding our temporal reality, we are compelled to form plans, strategize, and motivate ourselves with goals. This is to be expected and, according to the Scriptures, even encouraged (Proverbs 21:5), but the trouble lies in attempting to exert control over our own destinies rather than seeking wisdom from the Lord.

If our plans contradict the beautifully orchestrated plans of the Lord, then all our misaligned intentions will fail. The Lord's purposes will always prevail over human tactics and strategies. By seeking the Lord and understanding his divine will, we can have a mind like Christ which strives to obey the Father in every aspect of life. Only then can we know that our plans are wrought in wisdom and are in alignment with the master planner.

What plans have you made for your life?
Have you asked God to align
your mind and your desires with his?

Combat Loneliness

Two are better than one,
because they have a good reward for their toil.
For if they fall, one will lift up his fellow.
But woe to him who is alone when he falls
and has not another to lift him up!

ECCLESIASTES 4:9-10 ESV

Our God is a relational God who wants us to be part of his family. To emphasize his love for companionship, he created marriages and families to represent a picture of himself and his heart for mankind. Having a spouse offers immense benefits to our physical and spiritual walk. In life, we have someone with whom we can share responsibilities, be intimate, and raise a family. With regard to our spiritual walk, our spouses can help keep us accountable, be a safe place and comfort when the woes of this world press down, and lift us back up when we stumble.

Together under the blessing and direction of the Most High, couples can combat loneliness, pray for each other, and help refine the gifts from God that they have seen in each other's characters. It is beyond a doubt better to have a companion to walk through life with than to attempt to make it alone.

Besides your spouse, who walks with you through life?

With Passion

Put on then, as God's chosen ones, holy and beloved, compassionate hearts, kindness, humility, meekness, and patience.

COLOSSIANS 3:12 ESV

We associate passion with marriage, but compassion? Yes. Compassion literally means *with passion*. Compassion is more than a strong emotion; it compels us into action to alleviate another's sorrow or suffering.

Some people are compassionate by nature. Most of us, however, find our compassion thermometer hovering close to zero at times. In marriage, we have endless opportunities to practice compassion. When our spouse has a headache or comes down with the flu, the natural response is to get out the Tylenol and make sure he or she can rest comfortably. But if our spouse contracts a debilitating disease? Can compassion walk that long road, day after day, year after year? If that day comes, we can count on God's enabling grace to fill us with his compassion. God doesn't expect us to serve with only our strength, and that is our greatest encouragement.

Have you shown compassion when your spouse had a bad day?
What practical things can you do
to alleviate each other's afflictions?

Dissonance

What harmony is there between Christ and Belial?
Or what does a believer have in common with an unbeliever?
2 CORINTHIANS 6:15 NIV

Who or what we associate ourselves with every day influences our beliefs and worldview. Many believers associate this verse with marriage, discouraging holy matrimony between two people who do not share the same faith. It does stand to reason that something as bonding as a marital union will be strained if only one person is following Christ, and the other is not because the two will be traveling in different directions. Paul's warning is broader than marriage, however.

The wisdom found here can be applied to any relationships which necessitates the kind of camaraderie that shares an end goal and a moral path to it. If two or more people do not hold the same values or desire the same outcome, they cannot achieve nearly as much as those who agree on the purpose and the execution. For anything to get done, there must be unity of values and vision. We will have trouble if there is misalignment, and this is the heart of Paul's warning about light and darkness. They are not compatible since they are at odds with each other.

What are some examples of healthy relationships
between believers and unbelievers?
Which relationships would cause disharmony?

Choosing Contentment

Not that I speak from want,
for I have learned to be content
in whatever circumstances I am.

PHILIPPIANS 4:11 NASB

Wouldn't it be nice if contentment were automatic? Life would be more pleasant, and we would be too! The hard truth is that contentment is a choice, but it is one we can all make. Even the apostle Paul admitted he had to learn how to be content.

Contentment is a by-product of accepting what you cannot change. It does not mean you agree with the way things are or that you like the way things are. Rather, it is a statement of faith. You acknowledge your circumstances while trusting God to change what you cannot change, and you accept what he sees fit to change. Then, you can rest, and inner conflicts cease.

Is there a circumstance in your lives
that you cannot change but would like to?
Can you choose to be content in this situation?

Undeserved

Bear with each other, and forgive each other.
If someone does wrong to you,
forgive that person because the Lord forgave you.
COLOSSIANS 3:13 NCV

In light of all we have been forgiven for it seems petty not to extend forgiveness to others. We have been forgiven of all our sins and the death consequence they required! In response, we are called to forgive others. As simple as it sounds, forgiving others is difficult. Our flesh cries out for justice, and often justice is delayed. Regardless of whether a friend insults you, a stranger robs you, a government official says something that offends you, or your own spouse cuts you down, the task of every Christian is to repay evil with good. Another person's sin does not allow for sin to be returned.

Because we have been forgiven much, we can also forgive much. Where someone may be weak, we should bear their burden. Praise God for his forgiveness, mercy, and love both for us and for others.

Who do you struggle to forgive?
Why do you think that is?

Unchained

Forget the former things;
do not dwell on the past.
ISAIAH 43:18 NIV

Israel was in captivity. Again. Their history was rich with wonder and miracles of how God freed them from the Egyptians, led them through the desert, granted them the Promised Land, and continued to redeem them again and again from their enemies. Yet their greatest enemy, the devil, continued to torment them. Their greatest captor was their own sin with which they could be charged as guilty.

By his unfathomable love, God had a plan of redemption for them from that too. Isaiah was not instructing them to forget their pasts in the sense of erasing from memory all the wonderous ways Yahweh had already delivered them. He was saying that in comparison to what Yahweh had coming for them still, the past was not even worth dwelling on! The best was yet to come, and they should keep their perspective forward. We are encouraged to do the same. We don't want to forget the many blessings of God, but we can put aside the disappointments in life and move forward.

*Do you anticipate greater things from God still
to come than you have already seen play out in your life?*

Mine

My lover is mine,
and I am his.

SONG OF SOLOMON 2:16 NLT

Marriage is not just a mutualistic relationship; it is synergistic, meaning it is greater than the sum of its parts. It is a union of a man and a woman with God at the center, in which both spouses are built up by each other to be better than they are alone. Marriage is a giving over of oneself, in a state of complete vulnerability and trust.

Just as Jesus committed himself to God's will by living a life on earth and dying on the cross for the sake of his bride, so a man is asked to give his all to protect and care for his wife. Just as the church is called to fully deny itself and follow the loving instruction of the Almighty, so a wife is encouraged to give herself completely to her husband. In a God-ordained marriage, both husband and wife can trust that their self-denial will be met with tender and unselfish love.

How can you be more vulnerable with each other?
How can you meet your spouse's vulnerability
with a Christ-like attitude?

Command and Promise

"Do not fear, for I am with you;
do not be dismayed, for I am your God.
I will strengthen you and help you;
I will uphold you with my righteous right hand."

ISAIAH 41:10 NIV

Isaiah's message to Israel was both a command and a promise. They had reason to be afraid – they lived during a stormy period when their sin was leading them on a fast track to judgment and captivity. Yet, God had not forsaken them. His judgment was coming, but so was his mercy. One day he would deliver them as he had their ancestors long before.

This command and promise is for us too. Our cultures are being taken captive spiritually. Blatant disobedience to God's Word is leading us further from God and closer to the enemy. These are tumultuous and potentially fearful times. We don't need to fear because God is with us and he will give us the strength we need to make it through.

As you see your nation turn increasingly away from God,
are you fearful?
Take some time to search the Scriptures
for more promises of God's protection, help, and strength.

Overflowing

"Give, and it will be given to you. A good measure, pressed down, shaken together and running over, will be poured into your lap. For with the measure you use, it will be measured to you."

LUKE 6:38 NIV

The imagery of Christ pouring blessings into our laps comes from the ancient Middle Eastern grain market. People went into the market and literally bought a lapful of grain! A part of their garment was folded up and secured by a sash, and the pocket created held the grain, filling their laps. The crowd listening to Jesus would have understood the illustration completely.

Many years ago, a young couple discovered this verse and decided to put it to the test. Having nothing to give away, they prayed that God would channel some money in their direction so they could pass it on. Within a week or so, a friend handed them $15 for no reason at all, just as a gift. They quickly gave it away. Within three weeks, they received the equivalent of $630 from various sources. Amazed and grateful, they learned a life lesson that we can learn, too. God wants to pour out his blessings on us, but our own generosity is the trigger. We do not give to get, but we also cannot out-give God! He will bless us as we bless others.

Would you consider yourselves a generous couple?
Are you willing to put God to the test and sacrificially give?

A Guard

Set a guard, O Lord, over my mouth;
keep watch over the door of my lips!

PSALM 141:3 ESV

The mouth can lead the rest of the body in a direction it should not go. Our words betray our thoughts, but they also help shape the thoughts of others. Imagine a child overhearing certain phrases that become lodged in the memory until those phrases become what the child believes. Or consider words spoken in the heat of a moment that do damage and cannot be recanted.

King David knew that he needed the Lord's help to guard his mouth. He had found his way into trouble because of words spoken in haste and in passion, so he sought the Lord and requested his help. All of us need help from the Lord to overcome our sinful tendencies and become more like Christ. The Lord Jesus was intentional, kind, and true in every word he spoke. What's more, he knew when to speak and when to remain silent. As we circumvent communication casualties, we need to ask the Lord to guide us in wisdom and truth so the words we utter bring life, truth, peace, and encouragement to those who are listening.

Are you cautious about your words
and how they might impact those around you?

Full Acceptance

Accept one another, then, just as Christ accepted you,
in order to bring praise to God.

ROMANS 15:7 NIV

There is a deep need in the human heart for acceptance. The longing to belong is a powerful, significant factor in our choices. Outside of Christ, it can lead us down the wrong path. In Christ, the need for acceptance is satisfied—not by our own striving, but through the relationship we have with the one who fully accepts us.

In Romans 15, Paul spoke to Jews and Gentiles, two groups of people who were polarized by culture and background. The Jews, God's chosen people, believed that Christ came exclusively for them, and they had difficulty accepting Gentile Christians into their fellowship. Paul urged them to accept one another just as Christ had accepted them. The message to us is the same! As believers, can we love and accept those in the Body of Christ who are radically different than we are? Jesus said our love for each other would cause people to be drawn to him.

*Is it difficult for you to accept others who look different,
have different backgrounds, or express different tastes?
Do you have difficulty accepting each other just as God
created you, or are you intent on changing one another?*

Where Wisdom Is

"The fear of the LORD—that is wisdom,
and to shun evil is understanding."

JOB 28:28 NIV

Unlike every other religious adherence on the planet, we have been given free grace that we did not—could not—earn. It is not dependent on our obedience or virtue. We obey the Lord because we love him and are grateful for what he has done for us. We also obey him out of reverence to his holy name.

If we truly understood even a sliver of how majestic the Lord is, it would fill us with such a holy fear that we would have an entirely new perspective and we would be overjoyed at the fact that we can serve him! This is where wisdom begins. A wise perspective recognizes that the point of all things is the Lord. When we truly understand the goodness of God and properly fear his authority, we wisely choose his way over our own. Our goodness only exists because of him.

God explained to Job that humans are willing to search high and low for treasures and riches, but hardly anyone searches for wisdom even though it is freely given. Why do you think that is?

September

God created mankind in his own image,
in the image of God he created them;
male and female he created them.

GENESIS 1:27 NIV

Ask for Wisdom

Know also that wisdom is like honey for you:
If you find it, there is a future hope for you,
and your hope will not be cut off.

PROVERBS 24:14 NIV

Wisdom must be present in every marriage. In order to make good choices, we need to contemplate choices in a godly manner and trust in the hope of our future. From day one of our marriages, there are decisions that will affect our lives in the near future and beyond.

Asking God for wisdom should be part of every couple's daily routine. In your quiet time together, ask God to grow your love for each other, to provide for and protect you as a couple, to draw you closer to him, and to lead you to wise choices that honor him. While decision-making is not always fun, choices must be made every day. Some are very small; others are monumental. All require wisdom to assure you choose God's way for your marriage and life.

When making decisions,
do you pray together about the right choice?
Do you search God's Word for answers?

Eternal Futures

We do not lose heart. Though outwardly we are wasting away, yet inwardly we are being renewed day by day. For our light and momentary troubles are achieving for us an eternal glory that far outweighs them all.

2 CORINTHIANS 4:16-17 NIV

*P*aul was no stranger to suffering. Having been beaten with rods, pelted with stones, thrown in jail, shipwrecked, and stranded, Paul's body must have truly looked like he was wasting away. His inward strength, however, was only increasing and renewing throughout every hardship he encountered. His strength came from the Lord, and his assurance from God's promises. He knew that regardless of how great his suffering was, it did not even compare to the eternal glory waiting for him.

Everything around us that vies for our attention or attempts to intimidate us is only temporary. One day, it will all fade away and only what is grounded in God will remain. That is the hope we have been given and the reward we persevere for. Be careful not to become engrossed with your temporary, physical appearance. It is what God is doing inside our hearts that counts because only that will remain.

Do you spend more time working on how you are perceived by others or on the condition of your heart before your Maker?

Hope and Mercy

Blessed be the God and Father of our Lord Jesus Christ! By his great mercy
he has given us a new birth into a living hope through the resurrection
of Jesus Christ from the dead.

1 PETER 1:3 NRSV

We deserve death, but God showed us mercy by withholding our due punishment and paying the price of our sins himself. This ultimate sacrifice and incredible display of love is worthy of our praise and obedience. The best way to praise God for his abundant mercy is through how we live. Our actions and choices reveal what is in our hearts.

If we truly grasp the magnitude of the freedom we were gifted, then our hearts would be flooded with love and gratitude. This, in turn, would reveal itself through us by the way we act toward others and how we navigate life's rocky paths. Through Christ's death and resurrection, we have been given a living hope that will not die or be disappointed. We cannot stay silent or passive about a hope that saved us from death and promised us a life forever with our Maker.

How is your attitude toward your spouse impacted
by the mercy and grace you receive from the Lord?

You First

Humility is the fear of the LORD;
its wages are riches and honor and life.
PROVERBS 22:4 NIV

*M*arriage is a perfect practicing place for humility since the Lord constantly calls us to serve each other and put our spouse's needs before our own. Regardless of whether our spouses seem worthy of our love and service or not, we give it to them because we owe it to God. Humility leads to understanding, which leads to a fear of the Lord, which leads to wisdom. A wise person will recognize the richness of walking with the Lord. Those who are wise are often also honored and respected. They find greater peace and contentment in life because their assurance is in God, and this leads to a better quality of life.

Our marriages will benefit greatly from walking in wisdom, which starts with humbly serving the needs of the other and loving them in a way that brings glory and praise to God. We were loved when we were utterly undeserving, and we can choose now to love our spouses because of our great love for God and the gift of marriage that he has entrusted us with.

What does your spouse need help with today?
How can you serve as if serving the Lord himself?

Pride or Honor

Pride brings a person low,
but the lowly in spirit gain honor.
PROVERBS 29:23 NIV

Pride was what manifested in Lucifer, the angel of light. The desire to be worshipped led to his fall from heaven. Pride is a preoccupation with serving ourselves and inevitably leads to greed, stubbornness, jealousy, and rebellion. We cannot serve two masters who have separate agendas. Often God will lead his children places they do not want to go or ask them to do things they do not want to do.

If we are infatuated with ourselves and slaves to our own desires, we cannot serve God in the moments is really matters. If our spirits are submissive and humble, we will recognize our King's voice and find joy in following him. This path leads to great honor because there is nothing more worthy than to spend our lives serving our Savior! The kingdom of God is paradoxical; he brings low those who attempt to elevate themselves, and he bestows honor on the lowly and obedient. It is in the heart of every person to desire recognition and respect, but we can allow God to bring those in his time and in his way. By chasing them, we lose sight of what truly matters.

What does it mean to be lowly in spirit?

Ability

We are not saying that we can do this work ourselves.
It is God who makes us able to do all that we do.

2 CORINTHIANS 3:5 NCV

As soon as we begin to find our confidence in ourselves, we start to drift off the path. Our strength and our skills are pathetic in comparison to the might of the Lord. It is God who makes us able to act righteously, resist temptation, and stay our course.

When Paul penned these words, it revealed his changed heart. As someone who had previously prided himself on his own merit, he had in time discovered his complete inability, and fallen to his knees before his Creator. He wrote that of all people, he had the most he could boast in. He was zealous, righteous, blameless, and came from a perfectly religious background and upbringing. And yet he came to realize that all his worthiness could not save him, nor help him to accomplish his mission. It is only by the strength of God that we live, and we rejoice in that.

What has God laid on your heart
to do that seems too great for you?
Have you asked him to give you strength to accomplish it?

You Before Me

Don't be selfish; don't try to impress others.
Be humble, thinking of others as better than yourselves.
PHILIPPIANS 2:3 NLT

When we live for the goal of impressing others, there is no room for unity and love. The two different ambitions do not coincide, so we are faced with a decision: us or others. Denying selfishness and choosing to serve other people requires humility. Humility comes from a proper perspective of who we are and who God is.

When we realize how wonderful God truly is, our perspective should change to one of joyful service rather than self-focus. How empty is a life which revolves around the glorification of self? Rather than waste our efforts on worthless attempts at others' approval and applause, we ought to keep the bigger picture in mind. Joining together with God to serve other people and allowing our lives to be a form of worship to him is far more fulfilling and lasting than any conceited promotion of ourselves.

Do you think of your spouse as better than yourself?
How can you practice putting them first?

Tears of Laughter

Then our mouth was filled with laughter,
and our tongue with shouts of joy;
then they said among the nations,
"The LORD has done great things for them."

PSALM 126:2 ESV

How remarkable to know that Jehovah God, the Almighty of the universe cares so much for us that he enjoys seeing us happy and rejoicing. Jehovah does not need us, and yet he derives pleasure in giving us joy. Because of his love, we have life and a hope for the future. God's Son, Jesus, perfectly imitated his Father's unselfish love by giving his perfect life as a ransom for us.

We are also made in the image of God and can reflect his qualities. In doing so, our experience is that when we give others a reason to laugh, a reason to shout joyfully, and do kind things for them, we bring happiness not only to them, but also to ourselves. Seek each day to make your spouse, your family, and your friends happy and joyful. Strive to pursue the best interests of others and you will always be rejoicing.

What great things has the Lord done
for you and your spouse lately?

People of Integrity

I know that you are pleased with me,
for my enemy does not triumph over me.
Because of my integrity you uphold me
and set me in your presence forever.

PSALM 41:11-12 NIV

David knew where his help came from. He did not attribute his numerous victories to himself but to the power of God. Confidence that God was pleased with him was evidenced in the fact that David's enemies were unable to overthrow him. The Lord had always protected and provided for David, and David always gave God the glory. As virtuous as he was, David still realized that his goodness and integrity were not enough to sustain him. It was the Lord alone who upheld him, and only by God's greatness was David able to accomplish all that he did.

More than anything else in the world, David proclaimed loud and often that he wanted to be in God's presence. This mattered more to him than all the kingdoms of earth. His pure desire to be close to God was why God referred to him as a man after his own heart. In fact, the tense that David used while scribing this psalm was present, stating that he knew he was already in God's presence. It wasn't a hope he had for the next life, but a reality he clung to in his daily life on earth.

How do you know that God is pleased with you?

Yes and No

Do not swear, either by heaven or by earth or by any other oath,
but let your "yes" be yes and your "no" be no,
so that you may not fall under condemnation.

JAMES 5:12 ESV

Since we are children of the Father of truth, our words should reflect it. God does not deceive, and he instructs us to be honest in all our dealings as well. It was common practice in the time of Jesus and James to make oaths as a way of convincing someone that you will uphold a certain deal or that what you were saying was true. If someone must swear on something that they are being truthful, they might not resemble a trustworthy person.

Honesty and integrity should be trademark features of a Christian since we represent our Father. Our characters and past dealings should be enough to reassure people that what we say is true and what we promise will be delivered. There should be no need to swear since we are already known to be dependable people. Living up to this standard is both necessary and different from the world around us which is why James thought it necessary to echo these profound words of Christ.

*Do people believe you when you tell them something
or do they dig for further reassurance?*

Follow Me

"Come, follow me,
and I will show you how to fish for people!"
MATTHEW 4:19 NLT

When Jesus came to earth, he came in human form to interact with humans. The messages he brought were of heavenly truths, but he used analogies and explanations which were easier for us to understand. It was common in those times for rabbis to go out and select the mentees they would like to accompany them in their teaching careers, so Jesus similarly went forth to find his disciples. Rather than searching the synagogues, however, he approached impressionable fishermen. His selection was truly "salt of the earth" workers who held no authority within the religious circles of society. When he approached them, he spoke a language that made sense to them.

Peter and Andrew knew what the Teacher meant when he said, "Come, follow me." They understood that he was calling them to a different life than they had ever imagined for themselves. Then he said, "I will show you how to fish for people." He was calling them to not simply feed people with fish anymore, but to reach them with the truth of the gospel message, which would feed them forever.

*Why is it important to meet people where they are,
and use terms they can understand?
Can you set aside Christian lingo long enough
to have a conversation about God that is understandable
to an unchurched person?*

Many Advisers

Without counsel plans fail,
but with many advisers they succeed.

PROVERBS 15:22 ESV

Our lives are comprised of a series of choices: what to study, where to work, who to marry, where to live, whether to have children, what to believe, and so forth. Relying on our own insight offers us only one perspective which is a very limited view. The Lord does not need counsel since he is both omniscient and omnipresent. However, we are human and subject to err.

As a married couple, we have the benefit of a partnership already available for creating and modifying plans, but there is wisdom in numbers. Along with our spouses, we should seek wise counsel from trusted and godly friends. Fools rush forward, but the wise exercise patience and a willingness to listen. God made us to need each other, and we are more likely to succeed with a wider perspective. No human has all the answers, but by heeding the warnings of others, we have far better odds of avoiding potential pitfalls and unforeseen dangers.

Who do you go to for advice?

Constructive Criticism

If you listen to constructive criticism,
you will be at home among the wise.
If you reject discipline, you only harm yourself;
but if you listen to correction,
you grow in understanding.
PROVERBS 15:31-32 NLT

Many people struggle to receive criticism because it feels demoralizing. For the sake of others, we should learn how to deliver truth and criticism in a helpful way and not a harmful one. By going the extra step to ensure a kind delivery, we stand a greater chance of our message being received and effecting change.

We should also make it our objective to be able to receive criticism well because through it we can correct our mistakes and continue to mature. This humble acceptance of truth, even when it stings, will lead to wisdom and understanding. Discipline is an act of love from the Lord who desires us to grow and reach our full potential. Similar to correction, discipline can either be accepted or rejected. Accepting it helps us learn from our pasts and improve, but rejecting it only stunts our growth and reveals our folly. If we want to become more like Christ, it will require that we learn to embrace correction and discipline.

Why is criticism difficult to receive?
Have you learned to give and receive criticism well
with your spouse?

Brotherly Affection

Love one another with brotherly affection.
Outdo one another in showing honor.
ROMANS 12:10 NLT

*D*o people describe you as a hugger? Affection comes more easily to some than to others. However, it is important to remember that genuine affection is not limited to physical touch. The above verse from Romans is more about a deep care for one another, and that kind of love is visible when you put others first.

In marriage, being authentic about your affection means that you take into consideration what your spouse needs to experience your love. Each person has different affectionate needs, and you honor them by giving them that affection openly and honestly.

In what way do you most appreciate affection?
Share this with each other, so that you can both share love
that will reach the other where it is needed.

Maker Marked

> Woe to those who quarrel with their Maker, those who are nothing
> but potsherds among the potsherds on the ground.
> Does the clay say to the potter, "What are you making?"
> Does your work say, "The potter has no hands."
>
> ISAIAH 45:9 NIV

Have you ever watched a potter work? The clay starts as a lump and doesn't look like much until time and careful molding takes hold. The process is messy for a long time, and the final product looks nothing like the beginning.

The same is true in our lives. At times, you wonder how God is molding you. You may question why your lives look messy, why your marriage is a little rough, and where God is in the midst of it. Remember that you are the clay, and the master potter knows what he is doing. He makes all things beautiful in his time.

Are you questioning where God is right now
or why your lives look the way they do?
Talk with your spouse about what is messy in your marriage.

Celebrate Often

Enjoy life with the woman whom you love all the days of your fleeting life which he has given to you under the sun; for this is your reward in life and in your toil in which you have labored under the sun.

ECCLESIASTES 9:9 NASB

This is a beautiful reminder from the designer of marriage, God himself. God loves to see our marriages thrive and to be enjoyed. Sadly, as years go by, some marriage mates drift apart. Should we give up on the wife or husband of our youth? Or do we work to improve the situation so that we can enjoy life with our spouses again?

Worldly advice tells us that we could look to another person for happiness if we have problems with our spouse. Is it wise to follow your own heart on this matter? Instead of following our hearts, we are told to safeguard them above all else because they are deceitful and wicked. Truly then, how much wiser to keep our hearts and minds clean from any thoughts of abandoning our marriage. Do you trust that what Jehovah says about life and marriage is true? Then by all means, guard against wrong thinking, stick closely to your spouse, work hard to improve anything that needs attention, and you will definitely enjoy life.

Do you believe that following our loving and wise Creator will result in happiness?

Eternal Blessing

May the LORD bless you and protect you.
May the LORD smile on you
and be gracious to you.
May the LORD show you his favor
and give you his peace.

NUMBERS 6:24-26 NLT

What does blessing really look like? We try to find God's blessing in our finances, in feeling comfortable, or in experiencing happiness in our relationships, but those are worldly blessings. Bank accounts can empty, and arguments are part of life. What can we do when earthly blessings fail us?

The Scriptures say that God's blessing is found in his protection, in his grace, and in his peace. While his blessings can be found in our homes and jobs, it is always found in his Word. Turn to him on your own and as a couple, and he will give you true peace.

Do you see God's blessings around you each day?
Share them with your spouse.

Good Works

We are His workmanship, created in Christ Jesus for good works,
which God prepared beforehand so that we would walk in them.

EPHESIANS 2:10 NASB

We spend a great deal of time dreaming about our futures and
what God wants us to do with our lives. As a couple, we can often
find ourselves asking the same questions over and over again. What
is God's next step for us? What is his calling for our lives? How do
we move forward together?

Ephesians is clear; we were created for good works. While we can
work for God as individuals, we can apply this to our marriages too.
God crafts spouses into one tool, each person bringing different
talents to the table. Together, couples can do good works for God
that they could not do alone.

What does "good works" mean to you as a couple?
Are you involved in doing these things?

Unique Gifts

In his grace, God has given us different gifts for doing certain things well. So if God has given you the ability to prophesy, speak out with as much faith as God has given you. If your gift is serving others, serve them well. If you are a teacher, teach well.

ROMANS 12:6-7 NLT

In a marriage, we cannot pretend to be something or someone that we are not. It is often said that our spouses see our best and our worst, and there is comfort in that. We need to be ourselves with the one who loves us the most. Our spouses encourage and advise us with full knowledge of our gifts and weaknesses.

In the same way, we cannot hide ourselves from our Creator. He fashioned our gifts, and he knows where we should use them. Be confident in your design. To rephrase this Scripture: do your gift well!

Discuss your gifts with each other.
Are you doing the things that represent who you really are?
Brainstorm together on how you can use
your individual talents for God.

Power in Weakness

"My grace is all you need. My power works best in weakness." So now
I am glad to boast about my weaknesses, so that the power of Christ can
work through me. That's why I take pleasure in my weaknesses, and in the
insults, hardships, persecutions, and troubles that I suffer for Christ.
For when I am weak, then I am strong.

2 CORINTHIANS 12:9-10 NLT

It is hard to appear weak, but the truth is we are all inadequate
humans already. When we recognize and admit our weaknesses,
both to God and to each other, we can begin to grow in them and
mature. Our shortcomings are no surprise to God; he is aware of
them and still chooses to use us for his glory. It is in our fallen state
where God meets us and draws us to himself!

Instead of attempting to be strong on our own, our only hope is
to approach the Lord in our weak and frail state, requesting his
strength to compensate and make us whole. He willingly gives us
what we need, and the process is so much smoother when we do
not try to fool ourselves and others with false airs of grandeur. Our
spouses, more than probably anyone else, are well acquainted with
our weaknesses, so any attempt to cover them up may only produce
feelings that are ingenuine. It would be better to help each other in
our weaknesses and look to each other for strength.

Do you respond to your spouse's weaknesses
with contempt or with kindness?

Family Support

Children are a heritage from the LORD, offspring a reward from him.
Like arrows in the hands of a warrior are children born in one's youth.
Blessed is the man whose quiver is full of them.
They will not be put to shame when they contend
with their opponents in court.

PSALM 127:3-5 NIV

There are many ways in which our Father showers us with blessings, and children is one of those ways. We cannot create life; only God can do that. He uses us as vessels to bring forth children, and he entrusts us with their care. Having children, especially many of them, means more work, more bills, and more sleepless nights. But it also means more laughter, more love, and more cuddles. When they grow up, it means more people willing to help take care of us.

The Lord always provides for us, and sometimes he does so in ways we would not expect while we are simply trying to follow him. His Word makes it clear that he loves children, and that they are a reward from him. They are blessings which add value to our lives, not curses which steal from us. Even in the difficult days, we should remember this and treat them like the valuable heritage that they are.

Do you have children of your own or are there children
in your life who you love and care for?
What has God taught you through them?

Continual

They were continually devoting themselves to the apostles' teaching
and to fellowship, to the breaking of bread and to prayer.

ACTS 2:42 NASB

Spanning time and crossing cultures, the church has taken many different forms and faces. But the original functions of the church of Christ remain the same. Christians are to devote themselves to learning more about the Lord Jesus and his Word just as they always have. We are called to fellowship with one another—to offer strength and encouragement to the body of believers assembled as they worship the Lord together.

Similar to how the early Christians broke bread together and shared whatever they had with one another, we are expected to use what we have to help meet the needs of our brothers and sisters in Christ. Prayer is a bond between us and God and us to each other. Praying together is powerful because we go before God in agreement. It unifies the body when we pray for each other or with each other.

*Have you and your spouse found time
to pray to God together today?*

Strength in Numbers

If one can overpower him who is alone, two can resist him.
A cord of three strands is not quickly torn apart.
ECCLESIASTES 4:12 NASB

We were never intended to walk alone. It is the Creator's intention that we fellowship with one another, pray for each other, and share in the troubles of others. The enemy will try to deceive us or attack us when we are alone, just like a predator attempts to draw its prey away from the larger herd. By staying connected with others who share our faith and by asking for help when we need it, we surround ourselves with strength that the enemy has a harder time penetrating.

Marriage offers us a lifelong partner who can help support us in the bad times and laugh with us in the good times. We are stronger together. It is also important to have others as well that we can go to. We do not need to include them in all the details of our married lives, but we do need other perspectives and voices to help us stay on course.

Do you and your spouse pray for each other?
Who else is praying for you and for your marriage?

Encouraging Words

Worry weighs a person down;
an encouraging word cheers a person up.

PROVERBS 12:25 NLT

Worry is the enemy of faith. Worry forgets that Jehovah is in control, that he has been since the beginning of time, and that he will continue to be for all eternity. Our omnipotent Father is both willing and able to protect his children, and we have nothing to worry about. This does not mean that we should turn a blind eye on the realities of this world, nor that we put on a false front of being carefree.

We are supposed to care, but we cast our cares on the Lord and maintain focus. He is our rock, our light, and our path home. When worry overtakes us, we look to him for reassurance and receive it. If we see that others are becoming consumed with worry and with the anxieties this world produces, we should remind them of the greatness of God and of his perfect plan. Clearly we cannot avoid the trials and the evils of this world, but as we make our way together, let us never forget how powerful an encouraging word can be.

Do you know anyone who needs encouragement today?
How can you offer that to them?

Words that Wound

If you bite and devour each other,
watch out or you will be destroyed by each other.
GALATIANS 5:15 NIV

Just as living under the law is a waste of the freedom Christ Jesus gave us, living for ourselves is also a waste of our freedom. We have been called to a far greater existence than one which begins and ends with ourselves. Within our marriages, we can daily practice living for someone else. As soon as our intentions and actions become self-focused, blaming and demanding ensue.

Two people living for themselves together will assuredly cross paths when their desires do not align. However, two people committed to serving each other, attempting to outdo the other with love and honor, and resolute in their sacrificial love will be blessed beyond measure! Marriage is a powerful yet fragile gift that the Lord trusts us with. Our words can wound, but they can also empower. Decide to build up rather than destroy.

Have you exchanged any regrettable words with your spouse that you would like to make amends for now?

Choose Better

What pleases the LORD more:
burnt offerings and sacrifices or obedience to his voice?
It is better to obey than to sacrifice.
It is better to listen to God than to offer the fat of sheep.

1 SAMUEL 15:22 NCV

We might say that we work long hours so our family can live a comfortable life. We might say that we keep the house incredibly clean to ensure a peaceful environment. These are both true, but often we set our own ideas of what sacrifice means for our family, and we sound the trumpet when we think we have sacrificed enough!

Sacrifice looks different to each person. What might be a sacrifice for you is not for your spouse or child. We should look for God's appreciation above all else. When you are frustrated, take a moment. It may be that the Lord wants you to obey his command to love, rather than to work for it. Work is good, but love is greater.

What do you think you sacrifice for your family?
Discuss this together and consider whether
this is God's requirement or your own.
How does the Lord want you to serve?

Our Safe Place

A gossip betrays a confidence,
but a trustworthy person keeps a secret.
PROVERBS 11:13 NIV

*M*arriage should be a safe place where partners can confide in matters of the heart and openly discuss thoughts about anything: silly or serious. Each spouse must be the one person that the other can depend on.

Perhaps we are pretty good at keeping our private conversations private, but there are times when we might share intimate knowledge with those outside of our marriage. Talkative or not, any of us can slip up and reveal what we should not. God intends for marriage to be a safe place for our hearts, and many discussions don't need to be shared beyond that space. Let us actively work to keep our marriages intimate.

Are you able to open up with one another about most topics?
Do you feel like you can trust each other with your words?
Make sure your marriage is a safe place for each other.

Breaching a Dam

Starting a quarrel is like breaching a dam;
so drop the matter before a dispute breaks out.
PROVERBS 17:14 NIV

The book of Proverbs is filled with practical wisdom: a treasure trove of sorts for everyday life. This specific proverb is as straightforward as they come, although perhaps difficult in execution. Becoming engaged in an argument is not usually a pleasant experience. Depending on who the argument is with, emotions can flare up quickly and words may be exchanged that cause hurt to either or both parties, and it does not take much to escalate matters to this level.

It is such a common scenario which could be diffused if we would take notice of the wisdom in this verse. There is so much more to gain by refraining from an argument than asserting our opinions and winning it. The short-term advantage of coming out on top in an argument does not compare to the long-term damage sharp words will cause in a relationship especially in a marriage. The apt comparison to breaching a dam highlights the destruction which is sure to ensue downstream. So, before a quarrel even begins, it is better for us to take stock of what might happen if we insist on continuing down that road.

When you and your spouse break into a dispute,
do you consider whether the matter
could easily be dropped before engaging?

Like Honey

Kind words are like honey—
sweet to the soul and healthy for the body.
PROVERBS 16:24 NLT

A kind word goes a long way. It can have an immediate physical effect on the receiver. When someone shares a kind word with another, defenses lower and the recipient feels calmer. So many other positive feelings can ensue simply from an encouraging word spoken in kindness.

Worry and anger cause actual physical harm to a person's body. It can build up and fester, causing anxiety and illness. Caring compliments offer health and happiness to a person's body because they are uplifting and inspiring. They can remove doubt and suspicion, or they can reignite faith in truth and goodness. A word spoken in wisdom can help a person feel valued and accepted. Kindness is also incredibly contagious. A person who feels grateful for the kindness they have been shown is more apt to pass that kindness along. Words have tremendous travel power, and when issued in godly wisdom, they can pull people back from danger and into the light of Christ.

When you notice something positive about another person,
do you share it or keep it silent?
Have you asked God to help you discern
when a kind word should be spoken?

Collected Baggage

Cast your cares on the Lord and he will sustain you;
he will never let the righteous be shaken.

PSALM 55:22 NIV

A man took a long journey carrying an empty sack over his shoulder. Along the way he saw a rock on the path. He bent down to pick it up and placed it in his bag. He found another and then another. Along the way he filled that sack and staggered under its weight. He could hardly walk and his destination seemed further away than when he began. Did he need that heavy burden? No! The rocks had blocked his path and the man needed to remove them to reach his destination.

Is your marriage suffering under so much collected baggage? God wants to shoulder your burdens. He wants the two of you to be free from the hardship and pain of the trials you face and problems you encounter. Do not punish yourselves by carrying the load on your own. Allow the Lord to give you peace and happiness. He delights in blessing you with his assistance when you need help.

Do you hold onto your burdens?
Can you let the Lord take care of your problems?
Can you share grievances with God?

October

Love each other with genuine affection,
And take delight in honoring each other.

ROMANS 12:10 NLT

Clear Truth

Stand firm and hold to the traditions that you were taught by us, either by our spoken word or by our letter. Now may our Lord Jesus Christ himself, and God our Father, who loved us and gave us eternal comfort and good hope through grace, comfort your hearts and establish them in every good work and word.

2 THESSALONIANS 2:15-17 ESV

Paul wrote a warning to the Thessalonians to hold fast to what they had learned. He cautioned them against drifting from their love of God or becoming persuaded by false messages. Rather than outright lie to us, the enemy attempts to distort the truth and weave in lies. By causing us to doubt, he can methodically lead us away from our love of God. We need discernment and discipline in the Word to be able to thwart his schemes. By doing so, we will have the wisdom and power to stand firm for what we know and hold fast to the teachings which have been passed on to us.

Having faced intense persecution, the Thessalonians needed God's refreshing hope, comfort, and strength. Only by God's grace were they able to face every plight with confidence. Similarly, we must cling to his goodness whenever we feel hopeless, tired, or confused. All the sustenance and refreshment we need can be found in Jesus. He is our eternal comfort.

How can you and your spouse encourage each other to remain in the truth?

True Wealth

Be still before the LORD and wait patiently for him;
fret not yourself over the one who prospers in his way,
over the man who carries out evil devices!

PSALM 37:7 ESV

Have you and your spouse ever been in a situation where it seems like everyone else is prospering more than you? You've watched your friends wear their stilettos or power suits as they climbed the corporate ladder. You've seen photos from their exotic trips. And you've visited their gorgeous homes complete with fancy cars and gleaming boats in the garage. Meanwhile at your house, you're stretching the budget by eating beans and rice. Your cheap car is falling apart, and your home needs repairs.

Sometimes it's hard not to be envious. It's often difficult to understand when you're trying to serve God and your friends aren't. That's when we're wise to be still before God and to share our hearts with him. When we stop to think about it, we realize that we're the ones who are truly blessed. Our homes might be humble, but they're happy. Our trips might not be expensive, but they're filled with laughter and love. Our riches aren't in our possessions—they're in each other.

What makes you truly wealthy?
When's the last time you thought about
how rich you are to have each other?

Being Quiet

Be angry, and do not sin;
ponder in your own hearts on your beds,
and be silent.

PSALM 4:4 ESV

Feeling angry is not a sin, but we are responsible for our actions. Even when wrongs have been done against us, we have the option to do what is right. Approaching a difficult situation with an angry heart in the heat of the moment can lead to regrettable outcomes. However, taking time to think through the matter in a private place can bring clarity, so it is easier to address the offenses in a calm and collected state.

Knowing when to be silent and when to speak demonstrates wisdom and self-control. When we become angry at our spouses, it is important to not speak in wrath or try to break each other down. Instead, take the time necessary to calm down and refocus. Then it is easier to stay on point and hear the other person's perspective.

When something makes you angry, what do you need
in order to give it to God and refrain from sinning?

For Me

You are worthy, our Lord and God, to receive glory and honor and power,
for you created all things, and by your will they were created
and have their being.

REVELATION 4:11 NIV

Everything begins and ends with God. The existence of nature and animals is to worship him. The point of our lives is to worship him. Even the purpose of our marriages is to worship him. He is worthy of glory, honor, and power because nothing good exists outside of him! It is only by him that we exist, so it should only be for him that we exist as well.

If matrimony truly is a picture of how God loves his people, then we should approach it with that same sort of situational reference. Trying to derive our "fair share" out of a marriage or using the other person's shortcomings as justification for our own wrongdoings does not demonstrate a commitment to God. Marriage requires sacrifice, humility, and forgiveness in the same way Christ demonstrated for us when he accepted our payment for sin on the cross.

How can you glorify and honor God in your marriage?

Kindness Overflow

Show respect for all people:
Love the brothers and sisters of God's family,
respect God, honor the king.

1 PETER 2:17 NCV

When our spouses disappoint us, we are called to show them respect. When other Christians are acting shamefully, we are to love them even still. God will sometimes do things or allow things that we do not understand, but we should respond in obedience. Our words about those in authority over us should be honorable and reflective of how Jesus would respond.

We cannot control other people, but we can control our responses. We do not have to agree with our spouse, friends, or those in leadership over us, but we do have to act in a way that is befitting of a child of God. Showing kindness has more power to soften hearts and bring about change than any disrespectful rebuttal or confrontation made in anger. Our desire should be for godly change and growth, not simply to stake our claim and make our opinion heard.

*How can you continue to love and respect your spouse
when you disagree or are disappointed?*

Learn from Wisdom

Stand up in the presence of the aged,
show respect for the elderly and revere your God.
I am the LORD.

LEVITICUS 19:32 NIV

One of the greatest blessings about extended family is the opportunity to learn from those who have more experience than you. Many young couples are fortunate enough to have parents or grandparents who have been married fifty years or longer. Being in the presence of those enduring marriages gives others a chance to learn the secrets of making marriage last. Looking at couples who have been married a long time, you can see the love on their faces accompanied by the lines and wrinkles of experience.

As you build your marriage, draw from the tried and true wisdom of others. Copy the good things you see. Visit with those you respect and make note of their wisdom. God will bless your marriage and strengthen it when you do.

Are there those in your family
who have been married a long time?
Take them out to dinner and soak up their wisdom.

Honoring Parents

"Honor your father and your mother, so that you may live long
in the land the LORD your God is giving you."

EXODUS 20:12 NIV

God set up marriage as an institution where a man and a woman would leave their parents and start their own families. That doesn't mean that God wants us to forget about our parents—and he promises there are big benefits in honoring them. A smart couple will avail themselves of the wisdom their parents have accumulated over the years. They'll ask for and listen to sage advice that will keep them from making mistakes they don't have to make.

A wise couple will set aside time to go see their parents, to call them, or to lend a helping hand whenever needed. As the years go by and their parents begin to need assistance, husbands and wives should honor the lifetime of love and care their parents gave them by returning the favor. God says that if we'll honor our parents, we'll live long in the land. Let's determine that we'll look back with sweet memories instead of regrets.

How can you honor your mother and father?
Do you carve time out of your schedule to be with them?

All About Me

Each one of you also must love his wife as he loves himself,
and the wife must respect her husband.

EPHESIANS 5:33 NIV

Love and respect are basic desires of every human. It is easy to fall into the trap of withholding one or the other from our spouses as a way of controlling them or trying to force change. God's love for us, however, is unending. Although there may be consequences for wrongdoings, he does not withhold his love from us.

In marriage, we have been told to love and respect our spouses. We love them because of the incredible love we have been shown, and we respect them because they are made in the image of God. One of the most practical ways we can demonstrate love and respect to God is by giving it to our spouse. It is not our duty to decide if they are worthy of it; we are in a marriage covenant with them and, for better or worse, we must love and respect each other.

What makes your spouse feel loved?
What makes them feel respected?

Work Ethic

In all the work you are doing, work the best you can.
Work as if you were doing it for the Lord, not for people.

COLOSSIANS 3:23 NCV

*E*ven though we don't begrudge working to support our families because we love them, it's easy to become weary along the way. And sometimes when the drudgery of life piles on us, we end up not doing our best. We have a responsibility to do our very best. Little eyes are watching us, and it's especially important that we set a good example.

A good work ethic will make a huge difference in our homes and at our work places. Our attitudes make the biggest difference, especially if we work as if we are doing it for God. If he is pleased with our efforts, it's guaranteed that our spouses and bosses will be as well. There's a special joy that is experienced when we work to please God. Can you imagine how different our homes would be if that were the standard for all of our responsibilities?

How can our attitudes affect our work?
What difference does it make
when we do things as to the Lord?

Bearing Fruit

We continually ask God to fill you with the knowledge of his will through
all the wisdom and understanding that the Spirit gives, so that you may
live a life worthy of the Lord and please him in every way: bearing fruit in
every good work, growing in the knowledge of God.

COLOSSIANS 1:9-10 NIV

There's something beautiful about an apple orchard when the fruit
grows and ripens on the trees. Bright green leaves and branches
laden with glossy red fruit present a charming vignette and the hope
of apple pies, jelly, and fresh applesauce. There's also something
beautiful about our lives and marriages when we bear fruit
spiritually, continuing to grow in the knowledge of God.

A wise couple will ask the Lord for wisdom and understanding.
They'll listen to the whispers of God, and their goal will be to please
him in every way. It's a goal for each of us personally, but when we
have the opportunity to observe our spouses as they grow more like
Jesus, it's inspiring. And that provides a sweet hope for the future.

What can you do as a couple to help each other grow in Christ?
How does it make you feel to see your spouse serving God?

Clear Guide

The LORD has told you what is good,
and this is what he requires of you:
to do what is right, to love mercy,
and to walk humbly with your God.

MICAH 6:8 NLT

Although the Lord has freely given us forgiveness, he does not expect us to use his gift as a reason to act shamefully. Those who wish to follow God are called to live as he did. The Bible offers us a very clear guide as to how we are to conduct ourselves. Then, to demonstrate a godly lifestyle for us even clearer, God came to the world as Jesus Christ and lived a perfect life. Those whom Jesus was closest to and lived day to day beside were convinced of his Lordship by his wise words and his complementary lifestyle.

Just as the Lord Jesus taught us by his own life, we are to do what is right regardless of the outcome or of what the people around us are doing. We are to love mercy even when our minds scream for justice and we have been injured or insulted. We must leave justice in the hands of God and desire mercy. Casting aside pride, we ought to walk humbly with God. When we are near him and in reverent awe of his majesty, it is much easier to realize our own humble state.

How can you and your spouse encourage each other
to follow these three mandates?

A Trustworthy Heart

This is how we know that we belong to the truth
and how we set our hearts at rest in his presence.

1 JOHN 3:19 NIV

Love is how we set our hearts at rest in God's presence. In the same way that Jesus gave his life for us, we should be willing to do likewise for our spouses. When God blesses us with material possessions, that's awesome, but we should also have hearts that are tender toward others who are in need. One unexpected benefit about having a generous heart is that when our spouses see our love in action, it makes them love us even more.

It's great to express our love with words—and that's vital in a marriage—but when we put that love into action, it's powerful. We can't out-give God. It seems that the more we give away, the more we love each other, and the more God blesses us and our homes. Determine as a couple to love others and to help whenever you can. You'll never regret it.

How can you put your love into action?
How does it make you feel when you see your spouse
being loving and kind to someone else?

Marriage Foundation

*Let all that I am wait quietly before God,
for my hope is in him.*
PSALM 62:5 NLT

We cannot build our homes, jobs, or marriages on shifting sand. Our hope is only secure in the Father and in his promises. People will disappoint, status is not fulfilling, and our earthly homes are only temporary. All that will remain is what is rooted in Christ. Then when everything around us is uncertain, when injustice is rampant and evil is prevailing, and when those closest to us have let us down, our hope remains intact. Quietly, not in a concerned or questioning way, we wait for the Lord because we know what he says is true.

There is nothing in this world that has the power to steal our peace and our joy. No attempt of the enemy can derail our hope or lead us into doubt. For thousands of years the Lord has never failed to do exactly what he has said he will do, so we can turn to him for assurance and completely trust the truth in his Word.

What is your marriage founded upon?

Our Fortress

Truly my soul finds rest in God;
my salvation comes from him.
Truly he is my rock and my salvation;
he is my fortress, I will never be shaken.

PSALM 62:1-2 NIV

All around us, in media and in life, there are examples of people trying to find fulfillment in others. Although we are created to need one another, ultimate love and sustenance comes only from our relationship with God. Another human is unable to offer what our souls crave most because our souls were made to desire God. When he is not at the center of our lives, we become off-balanced and uneasy.

Our search to find fulfillment elsewhere will only lead us further off course until we admit the need for our Creator. In him, we find our rest and our internal calm. In him, we are grounded, centered, and focused. Nothing that comes against us can shake us because he is our immovable rock and the holder of our hearts. Salvation and safety can only be found in him.

What place does God have in your life?
What place does your spouse have?

Love Covers

Above all, love each other deeply,
because love covers over a multitude of sins.
1 PETER 4:8 NIV

*L*ove looks past the shortcomings of another and sees the person God created. Even though we have all failed many times, the God still loves us. In this same manner, he has instructed us to love each other deeply. This comes from the Greek word *ektenés* which is used to describe the strenuous activity of an athlete's muscles when sprinting.

Love is not easy, nor is it simply a feeling. Love is a commitment to choose each other amid the sins, failures, and disappointments. Marriage requires even more grace since the actions of our spouses directly affect us. Our love must be ardent and determined, not dependent on our feelings or the actions of our spouses. We must commit to love our spouses in the good times and the bad.

How can you show your spouse you love them
when you do not feel very loving?

Perfect Example

Husbands, love your wives,
just as Christ loved the church
and gave himself up for her.
EPHESIANS 5:25 NIV

The sort of love expected of husbands toward their wives is far greater than mere sentiment. If it were required, he should love her even to the point of death! Christ's sacrifice was so great that the imagery depicted in this verse should not be overlooked or undervalued. This is an active, sacrificial love that considers the needs of a wife over even his own.

Just as the wife is called to submit to her husband, the husband is similarly called to submit his own desires to the care and love of his wife. Christ gave us the perfect example of love, and now it is our responsibility and honor to replicate that example to each other, to the rest of our families, and to anyone else the Lord places in our paths.

*How can you apply your understanding of salvation
to your marriage?*

Truly Amazing

There are three things that amaze me—no, four things that I don't understand: how an eagle glides through the sky, how a snake slithers on a rock, how a ship navigates the ocean, how a man loves a woman.

PROVERBS 30:18-19 NLT

Of everything we experience, true love between a husband and wife is one of the strongest and most amazing experiences of all. We marvel at the power and elegance of an eagle gliding silently through the sky, its keen eyes searching far and wide. We are fascinated by creatures who must regulate themselves, carefully gauging their own bodies to know what is needed for optimal health. We are in awe of mighty ships that traverse even mightier oceans, with difficulties and peril on every horizon. How much more should we give thanks to our Creator for the wonderful and amazing gift of love between ourselves and our marriage mate?

Proper love for our spouses is even stronger than love of our own life. Like a powerful ship on a stormy sea, we must build each other up, work together as a team, and closely follow the commands of our loving Father. We need to keep constant watch over our marriages, making sure that things are kept in balance. And like the majestic eagle, if we keep our love pure and keenly look for ways to improve our marriages in Godly ways, we will soar above the problems that come our way.

*What signs does your spouse give you
that they need comfort and reassurance?*

More Important

Love is patient and kind.
Love is not jealous,
it does not brag,
and it is not proud.

1 CORINTHIANS 13:4 NCV

There's something built inside us that makes us want to brag: "Look what I did!" But what if we spent more time bragging about our spouses than we did about ourselves? That's where true love comes in. When we pay attention to others—especially our spouses—that means we're taking our eyes off ourselves.

Love is patient and kind. It's about giving up our own will for someone we love more. And it's not just about being there for our spouses during hard times, but also celebrating with and for them in good times—with no jealousy involved. What if God had been selfish? What if he'd said, "My life is more important than yours?" But he didn't, and wise husbands and wives will make it a goal to follow his example to love their spouses more than themselves.

What tangible thing could you do today
to love your spouse more than yourself?
What do you need to change?

Less of Me

"I can do nothing on my own. I judge as God tells me.
Therefore, my judgment is just,
because I carry out the will of the one who sent me,
not my own will."

JOHN 5:30 NLT

Husbands and wives often have great goals, but it usually doesn't take long for us to realize that our power to achieve those goals lies in God. We can't do anything without him. He is the source of our strength, and yet this all-powerful God is in love with us. His heart is touched when we want to do his will, when the desires of our hearts are to serve him.

When we seek to serve him our own desires are being put on the back-burner where they should be. It means less of self, and that's a good thing! In a home where a husband and wife are committed to doing God's will together and putting their spouse's needs before their own, the relationship will thrive.

*How can you be more selfless in your relationship
with your husband or wife?
How does it impact you
when you see your spouse being selfless?*

Racing Partner

Since we are surrounded by such a huge crowd of witnesses
to the life of faith, let us strip off every weight that slows us down,
especially the sin that so easily trips us up.
And let us run with endurance the race God has set before us.

HEBREWS 12:1 NLT

Racing with a partner can inspire us to push further than we would on our own. Having someone cheering us on is a great encouragement and motivator! Running alone is difficult, and sometimes a simple word of assurance can give us the courage we need to keep going in this hectic, overwhelming world.

As we strive to shake off the needless weights the world throws on us, we can lean on each other for help and strength. God gave us other people so we could run this race together. We ought to share both our helping hands as well as our burdens, continuing to race together.

*What are some practical ways
you can cheer your race partner on?*

No Callouses

"This people's heart has become calloused; they hardly hear with their ears,
and they have closed their eyes. Otherwise they might see with their eyes,
hear with their ears, understand with their hearts and turn,
and I would heal them."

MATTHEW 13:15 NIV

Have you ever been somewhere that was so loud you couldn't hear what your spouse was saying? Or somewhere the sun was so bright you had to close your eyes? Do you know that we sometimes do the same thing with God? He tries to communicate with us, but we've allowed our hearts to become calloused, and we close our ears or shut our eyes so we don't have to hear what he wants to tell us.

But if we want our homes and marriages to be healed, we have to be sensitive to his voice, we have to turn away from the things that he doesn't want us to do, and we have to give our hearts permission to understand. Let's determine that we will work to keep our hearts soft and sensitive to him.

How can our hearts become calloused?
How does that affect our marriages?

Loving Rebuke

Do not rebuke mockers or they will hate you;
rebuke the wise and they will love you.

PROVERBS 9:8 NIV

*R*ebuke is not a very modern word. But it is a strong word. There is nothing weak or pleasant about being rebuked. To be reprimanded in an angry or negative way can be devastating, especially to a sensitive person. When someone you love does something out of line, gentle, loving correction is a much better way. If you need a reminder you have overstepped boundaries, appreciate the one who loves you enough to bring you back into line.

We count on our mates for many things. Many are fun. But one of the things we need to be assured of is that our spouses will let us know when we need correction. Love will permeate the correction as we help our mates grow to become better people. Coming from one who loves us more than anyone else in the world, it makes us feel secure and helps to diminish feelings of rebellion and sensitivity.

Have you ever been rebuked by your mate?
Discuss those times and why
it was easier coming from him or her.

Peace through Laws

Great peace have those who love your law;
nothing can make them stumble.

PSALM 119:165 NRSV

When we receive God's forgiveness for our sins and declare that he is Lord of our life, we stop living for ourselves and we follow his leadership. This is accompanied by a set of rules and guidelines that God, in his lovingkindness, established so we could live a worthwhile life to the fullest measure! Begrudging compliance will not please either God or us. When we learn his laws, seek to truly understand why he instated them, and realize the good that comes from adherence, we end up loving them and experiencing unexplainable peace.

True to its depiction of the love of God, marriage operates in the same fashion. When we commit our lives to one person, many freedoms we previously experienced are traded in for the adventure of marital love and companionship. Suddenly, we answer to someone else and must lay our own wishes down. What matters now is a strong partnership rather than two individual sets of interests.

What binding elements of marriage have you learned to love?

Servant's Heart

He sat down and called the twelve.
And he said to them, "If anyone would be first,
he must be last of all and servant of all."

MARK 9:35 ESV

When Jesus taught his disciples what a true leader was, he used the Greek word *diakonos* which here is translated "servant." This word, from which we get the word *deacon*, means someone who attends to the needs and desires of another. Jesus demonstrated this style of leadership throughout his life and instructed his followers to do likewise.

In our lives, and especially in our marriages, we are to follow the example of Christ and become a servant of all. Like our Lord chose to do for the sake of those he loves, we have the privilege of laying aside our rights and our freedoms to help others. Issues within marriage hardly ever cut fair, so a more advantageous approach would be to love and serve our spouses whenever and however we can.

In what ways is God's kingdom a paradox
to how we understand worldly establishments?

Sharing

If you help the poor,
you are lending to the LORD—
and he will repay you!

PROVERBS 19:17 NLT

This psalmist captures a sliver of God's altruistic personality in this verse. The motion of lending to the Lord draws out the essence of God and the desire he has for his people. His very nature is caring, empathetic, and generous which is how he wants his children to also be. Making us aware of who he is teaches us how we ought to be. Those who are poor are so close to the heart of God that by giving to them it is as if we give straight to God.

Later in the New Testament, Christ clarified how he expects believers to love their neighbors as if they were loving themselves. He also told the story of the Good Samaritan which demonstrated the kind of care and compassion Christians are supposed to show anyone who is in need. Ultimately, the Creator is glorified when we actively love his creation. Not only is helping the poor a form of worship to God, it is directly tied into our God-given purpose—and he also repays those who give! God is faithful; he rewards those who diligently seek him. When we serve others, we become more like our Father and that is an unfathomable reward.

What can you do this week to help the poor?

Extending a Hand

Is not this the kind of fasting I have chosen: Is it not to share your food
with the hungry and to provide the poor wanderer with shelter—
when you see the naked, to clothe them, and not to turn away
from your own flesh and blood?

ISAIAH 58:6-7 NIV

Early marriage brings challenges: making ends meet, adjusting to
life as a couple, combining two sets of family values into one, and so
forth. One question may arise: how do we operate our family and
still be able to give to others? For some couples, it seems like there is
never enough extra to go around. But God directs us to help others
in whatever ways we can. In the beginning it may be small. In time
those ways will become bigger.

Find ways to share with others. Gifts of time, good used items, or
services are additional things you can do together. If your interests
are different, schedule one evening a week to serve in different
places. Offer your gifts as a sacrifice to God and enjoy the rewards of
serving him.

What would you like to offer to God as an act of service?

Sharing Eternity

"Anyone who has two shirts should share with the one who has none, and anyone who has food should do the same."

LUKE 3:11 NIV

Here we see the fine teaching of Jesus himself. What good things God has given us! We have life, a measure of health, and he gave us a beautiful earth as our home. When we reflect on our blessings, and the Bible's promises for a bright future, should we not feel compelled to be generous with our spiritual brothers and sisters? In fact, our heavenly Father expects us to show kindness and generosity. Our attitude in this matter directly affects our relationship with him.

Within the family of God, the Bible shows that the husband and wife are considered one flesh. If God expects us to show kindness, generosity, and affection for those who are related to us in the faith, how much more so does he expect a husband and wife to honor each other and give each other the emotional, material, and physical support they need? Thinking about the good things that Jehovah has given us should move us to give freely.

Is your spouse, family, friend, or neighbor
lacking something that you have the ability to fill?

Careful Words

If anyone speaks, they should do so as one who speaks the very words of
God. If anyone serves, they should do so with the strength God provides,
so that in all things God may be praised through Jesus Christ. To him be
the glory and the power for ever and ever.

1 PETER 4:11 NIV

Everything we have has been entrusted to us by God. Our wealth
and possessions as well as our opportunities and abilities. When
we open our mouths to speak, it should be to honor God and not
ourselves. All credit and praise are due to him. When others thank
us for our help, we ought to remember to thank God.

Similarly, our marriages are a gift from God, and we should
approach them with this sort of reverence. We cannot take our
spouses for granted or act as though we somehow deserve the
blessings that come through marriage. Our spouses are God's
children and he entrusted them to us. The words that we say and
the deeds that we do for them should demonstrate our gratefulness
to God for his gift and the respect we have for the position he has
placed us in. Words carry power, so let us use ours for God's glory
and not our own conceited agendas.

Do your words reflect your appreciation toward God?

Precious Promise

The God of peace will soon crush Satan under your feet.
The grace of our Lord Jesus be with you.

ROMANS 16:20 NIV

Stress can work havoc on a marriage. Becoming stressed is easy—getting rid of it is not. Overwhelming demands at work, health issues, trouble with kids and families, tension with spouses, lack of time with God, and exhaustion can all take a toll. And an over-stressed spouse can become snippy and impatient, further compounding the problems at home. So how do we get out of that pattern?

We can pray for our spouses, lifting their needs to the God who can fix them. We can help shoulder the burden. Two carrying a load is much better than one. We can provide tender affection and words of encouragement. And we can be spiritual helpers to our spouses, reminding them of God's sweet and precious promise of grace.

How can you help your spouse when he or she is stressed?
How has God's grace helped you in the past?

Part of the Equation

The human body has many parts,
but the many parts make up one whole body.
So it is with the body of Christ.

1 CORINTHIANS 12:12 NLT

To love each other as if we were one body requires a different perspective than the world teaches. In a culture which promotes entitlement, individualism, and pride, Paul counteracts such empty pursuits by challenging believers to consider who we are in Christ. If we have truly separated ourselves from our sinful natures and been grafted into God's family, then other believers are our family members. It is as if we are one body, and we need to care for each other as such.

Within a marriage where a husband and wife become one flesh, this is even more imperative. Marriage is meant to be a picture of Christ's love for us. When we begin putting the needs of our spouses before our own, we portray that image the way it was intended.

What can you do to care for the needs of your spouse today?

Better Days

God is our refuge and strength,
an ever-present help in trouble.
PSALM 46:1 NIV

In times of trouble it is easy to look back on better times. If you could only go back to the way things were earlier in your marriage. Back before you had children or lost your job, before the house got cluttered or your mother-in-law moved in. But were those *really* better times? Living involves moving in the present and on into the future. Our yesterdays may seem better or less hectic, but God has a future for us. Without going through trials or hard times we would face the days ahead without maturity and wisdom that comes through perseverance. Each test brings with it the ability to stay the course.

Worrying about the future will not benefit anyone. Together, the two of you can use your experience and expertise to safely navigate whatever bumps in the road you encounter. Trust that the Lord has your best interests at the center of his heart, and rely on his promises. Seek his wisdom and guidance.

Can you let go of worry?
How can you help each other to trust God in hard times?
What strengths do you see in each other
that have resulted from previous hard times?

November

If a man tried to buy love
with all his wealth,
his offer would be utterly scorned.

SONG OF SOLOMON 8:7 NLT

Ruling a Kingdom

LORD, the God of our ancestors, are you not the God who is in heaven? You rule over all the kingdoms of the nations. Power and might are in your hand, and no one can withstand you.

2 CHRONICLES 20:6 NIV

Does it ever feel like this world and its problems are too vast and intense? Injustice looms and threatens to overthrow our efforts. Sometimes the tragedies in our own lives seem like more than we can cope with, and other times we are devastated by news from far away. Yet amidst all the anguish stands a resolute promise, that the Lord is nearby and he hears the cries of the suffering. Nothing escapes his loving glance, and there is no adversary who can stand against him.

Although God may allow evil to reign for a time, giving us opportunities to follow him in faith, his ultimate plan will be enacted. We will be saved from everything which threatens to undo us. His kingdom is forever, and his judgment is sound. Within him is all power and all love! Even now he is holding us with his mighty hand, and although the threat seems strong, there is nothing that can separate us from his love. He has been guarding and upholding his people since the beginning of time and he is not going to change that now.

When you are feeling overwhelmed or dismayed, what Scriptures bring you comfort and encouragement?

Openness in Love

Better is open rebuke than hidden love.
Wounds from a friend can be trusted,
but an enemy multiplies kisses.

PROVERBS 27:5-6 NIV

A true friend cares more about you than they do your opinion of them. Sensitive matters must be addressed gently and respectfully, but truth should always be the prevailing word. A fragile friendship may crumble under offense, but when true love exists, it does not have to worry about the relationship being crushed by critique.

One who is self-seeking may use flattery to win attention from others, but their words are not based in truth or love. When hard times come or their own desires lead them elsewhere, they will be gone and with them their empty praises. Someone who sincerely loves will be open and forthcoming. They understand that the depth of the relationship requires honesty and integrity of speech. When someone who cares for us criticizes us with no personal gain achieved, we would be wise to listen and consider the matter.

How well do you receive criticism from your spouse?
How kindly do you offer it?

Inner Circle

Whoever walks with the wise becomes wise,
but the companion of fools suffers harm.
PROVERBS 13:20 NRSV

Every couple needs friends. These are the people who know us and love us. They are our confidants and counselors. They bring fun, companionship, and encouragement, and they serve God with us. Because friends are so influential, we need to be careful about who we bring into our inner circles.

God's Word says it best. If we want to be wise, we need to hang around wise people, and if we choose fools for our buddies, it will hurt us. Our friends impact us on many levels. If we hang out with people who are loose with their marriage vows, or are unloving and unkind to their spouses, that can rub off on us. But if we have friends who love God and base their relationships and daily lives around him, we are blessed by their example. Let us choose our friends wisely, and be godly friends for them in return.

Would God consider your friends wise or foolish?
As a couple, what safeguards can you set
to help you pick the friends of your inner circle?

A Reliable Friend

One who has unreliable friends soon comes to ruin,
but there is a friend who sticks closer than a brother.
PROVERBS 18:24 NIV

It is no secret that who we associate with has a tremendous influence on us. A person who proves to be unreliable should, clearly, not be relied upon. We can still care about this person, but it would be foolish to depend on them when difficult times come upon us because we will ultimately be led to ruin. They will not come through for us regardless of how much we love them or want to believe in their potential.

Trials reveal the true nature of people, and they can also divulge who are dependable friends. The loyalty and good nature of some people will spring forth during hardships, and these are the individuals who prove to be as dependable as our own families. A steady, trustworthy friend is worth more than riches because they will be there in the fun times as well as the bad. Their faithfulness and love can keep us from ruin, and we should strive to offer the same loyalty and consistency to them. These are the friendships worth fighting for.

Which of your friends would you turn to in an emergency?
Who would you look to for a true answer?
How were you able to identify these people?

God-Positioning System

In all your ways acknowledge Him,
and He will make your paths straight.
PROVERBS 3:6 NASB

Have you ever thought about how marriage is like a road trip? When we take our wedding vows, we start a long journey often without a clue about where we'll end up or how we'll get there. Is there a map? When we pack our families into our cars and head out for vacation, we have to trust our maps or our GPS to get us where we're going.

God's Word is life's GPS—our God-Positioning System. As we go through life, he takes us on some major twists and turns down roads that don't make sense to us. But we trust the one who's been down them before, who knows the pitfalls and dangers along the way. We need to acknowledge that he's the one in charge, trust him, and follow the path into the future that he has mapped out for us.

Why is it so hard to trust God
when we don't know where he's leading us?
As a couple, what have you learned
about trusting God in uncertain situations?

Cold Water

> "If anyone gives even a cup of cold water to one of these little ones who is my disciple, truly I tell you, that person will certainly not lose their reward."
>
> MATTHEW 10:42 NIV

Have you ever seen your spouse take food to a homeless person or dig into his pocket for money to help someone going through difficult times? Have you observed your sweetheart carrying a home-cooked meal to someone who's just had surgery or holding someone's hand as she prayed for them? Doesn't it make you love them even more?

God says he will reward us for our good works, but our marriage gains love from such moments of kindness too. There's something about generosity, about watching each other dispense compassion, that makes us love each other more. Why? We are watching our spouses reflect Jesus. It's even more special when we can share those moments together.

*Can you recall a time that your spouse
was compassionate to someone?
Is there something that you can do as husband and wife
to touch the lives of others?*

Unmerited Favor

The God of all grace, who called you to his eternal glory in Christ,
after you have suffered a little while, will himself restore you
and make you strong, firm and steadfast.

1 PETER 5:10 NIV

Grace is showing kindness when someone doesn't deserve it. It is unmerited favor. God gave us the perfect example of grace when, while we were still in sin, he gave his Son to die for us. We deserved death, but he gave us life. Christ's sacrificial, grace-filled relationship with his church is often compared to marriage.

Grace in marriage is essential. Overlooking when your spouse squeezes the toothpaste in the middle is grace. Not getting angry when your partner speaks harshly after a hard day is grace. Since God shows us grace, we can follow his example and give it freely to those we love.

*Where are some areas where you need
your spouse to show you grace?
Thank your spouse for a specific time
in which he or she was gracious.*

New Grip

Take a new grip with your tired hands and strengthen your weak knees.
Mark out a straight path for your feet so that those who are weak and lame
will not fall but become strong.

HEBREWS 12:12-13 NLT

Suffering is not enjoyable, but it is purposeful. Disciplining children helps them be able to self-discipline later in life. Since God is a good Father, he disciplines his children out of love. He is protecting us and maturing us. By embracing his correction and learning to say no to the things which are bad for us, we become stronger and we will not fall nearly as often.

Like an athlete trains for a game, if we expect to win, we must also buckle down and train. Take hold of what is good, strengthen yourself through prayer and obedience, and plan to do what you are called to do. We must actually mark out a straight path by determining to do the right thing and by avoiding obstacles. If we allow life to just happen to us and hope to avoid temptations and trials, we will succumb much more frequently than we will if we have a training plan in place.

*What actions can you and your spouse take
to mark out a straight path for yourselves?*

Blossoming

We all, who with unveiled faces contemplate the Lord's glory,
are being transformed into his image with ever-increasing glory,
which comes from the Lord, who is the Spirit.

2 CORINTHIANS 3:18 NIV

"She's not the same woman I married."

"He's changed."

These words have been uttered to many marriage counselors. The counselor's response is almost always the same.

"You are correct. Your wife isn't the same person you married, and your husband has changed."

Your experiences grow and change you. Imagine that you planted two trees on your wedding day, one to represent each of you. You would expect to see them gain height and breadth and blossom. Growth is a good thing. Don't expect your spouse to stay the same. Focus instead on how, when rooted in Christ, you can grow together.

How have you each changed since the day you married?
Can you tell what caused that change?
What remains the same?

Elementary Teaching

Leaving the elementary teaching about the Christ, let us press on to
maturity, not laying again a foundation of repentance from dead works and
of faith toward God, of instruction about washings and laying on of hands,
and the resurrection of the dead and eternal judgment.

HEBREWS 6:1-2 NASB

As we continue to grow in our relationship with God, our
understanding of him matures. We should not be mulling over
the same elementary teachings but diving deeper into his Word to
uncover more of his glorious mysteries.

After being married for years, you would not continue to ask your
spouse the same questions you did when first getting to know each
other; instead your conversations would consist of topics with more
depth, built on a foundation of understanding which has already
been laid. In the same way, our closeness to God is evidenced in
how we have sought him through prayer and reading, and how we
have carried out his instructions. This happens over time and takes
intentional interaction with the Lord.

Since we know that relationships do not stay stationary,
how can you pursue the Lord today?
How can you pursue your spouse?

Mature in Love

When I was a child, I used to speak like a child,
think like a child, reason like a child;
when I became a man, I did away with childish things.

1 CORINTHIANS 13:11 NIV

*I*n the past, we were children with time to waste and little responsibility. Most of us only needed to take care of ourselves. Our speech was childish, and our reasoning was limited. As we matured, however, we began to take on more responsibility. We talked less about childish fantasies and more about our daily responsibilities.

After we got married, we learned even more how to take responsibility for our choices, words, and actions since they directly affected someone very close and dear. In a healthy marriage, we continue to mature in love. Our capacity to care for someone else grows, and our love for the Lord extends even further. God is ready to bring us to new heights and open our eyes to his mysteries if we are willing to walk in obedience and lay aside our immaturity.

What is the difference between childish understanding
and child-like faith?

Artist, Builder, Writer

Do not neglect the gift that is in you, which was given to you by prophecy
with the laying on of the hands of the eldership. Meditate on these things;
give yourself entirely to them, that your progress may be evident to all.

1 TIMOTHY 4:14-15 NKJV

Do you ever think about the fact that God gave unique gifts and talents to each of us? Wise husbands and wives look for those skills in their spouses, and they help nurture and grow those interests. Is your wife a talented artist? Set aside a place in your home for her to paint. Is your husband gifted at building things? Buy him some tools or hang out at the building supply store with him. Does your spouse want to be a writer? Save your pennies and send him or her to a writer's conference.

Encourage each other. Give sincere praise. Pray about ways to use your talents for the Lord, and be the proudest one there when others are admiring your sweetheart's handiwork. Don't waste the gifts that are inside you. Work together as a couple to help them grow and flourish.

What are the special talents
that God has given to you and your spouse?
How can you encourage each other to use those gifts?

Better Balance

Grow in the grace and knowledge of our Lord and Savior Jesus Christ.
To him be the glory, both now and to the day of eternity. Amen.

2 PETER 3:18 NIV

In the final salutation of his letter, Peter left his readers with two tasks: to grow in the grace of Jesus Christ and to grow in the knowledge of him. To grow in grace does not mean to acquire more grace, since grace is given to us by God and we already have it to the fullest measure. Peter is encouraging us to grow and mature within the grace that has been provided to us.

When we truly understand how radical and thorough God's grace is, we can begin to live in the freedom that he gave us. Instead of focusing on our shortcomings and introspecting too much, we can rejoice in the grace allotted to us by Jesus Christ and gain a healthier perspective. Our focus can be on how to love God and serve other people, instead of sinking in our own insecurities. We are also to grow in our knowledge of Jesus Christ, which reveals God's heart and perspective. It is important to learn to see things the way God does rather than relying on our own limited views.

*What does growing in the grace of Jesus
look like in your marriage?*

Joined Together

"What God has joined together,
let no one separate."

MARK 10:9 NIV

Marriage is a sacred bond, ordained by God. It is a precious promise between a man and a woman: a lifelong vow that should be protected at all costs. But our wedding vows aren't magical words that make protection happen. We need to focus careful thought and attention on our marriages, and we need to be proactive about any negative influences that could creep in and crack our bonds. Without care, other people (including family members), outside influences, wandering eyes, and the like can impact our marriages and homes.

The God of the universe joined you and your spouse. Wedding vows aren't magic words, but your sacred union is better than magic. Shouldn't you both put forth the utmost effort to keep the world from destroying this priceless and irreplaceable gift? Work together to be a united front, keep your guard up, and work hard to keep the fire of your love burning.

What could cause division in your marriage?
What steps can you take
to protect your God-given relationship?

Don't Look Back

Let not your heart turn aside to her ways;
do not stray into her paths.
PROVERBS 7:25 ESV

There are many sins the Bible tells us to stand up to and fight against, to go forth in courage and overcome! When it comes to the issue of sexual sin, however, it always cautions us to run. Steer clear, do not look back, and avoid it at all costs. God created us to be attracted to other people, which is why marriage is such an incredible and powerful gift. Yet it also means it is easy to become ensnared in our lustful urges especially in a culture which freely propagates sensuality.

When we choose to follow our fantasies rather than our commitments, we scorn the gift God has given us and we hurt ourselves and our loved ones. The marriage bond is holy and deserves our loyal attention. Our love and commitment both to God and our spouses compels us to live a disciplined and chaste life, and we should not test our human natures by even flirting with the notions of adultery. It is never worth it.

What can you do when confronted with sexual temptation?
Have you adopted any habits or safeguards in your marriage
to help you choose purity?

Wisdom Granted

The LORD grants wisdom!
From his mouth come knowledge and understanding.
PROVERBS 2:6 NLT

To be with God is to grow in wisdom. James warns that self-seeking leads to confusion but when we seek God, he opens our eyes to the truth and we grow in our knowledge and understanding of how things really are. There are many pursuits in this world that captivate the hearts of mankind, but our heavenly Father should be our greatest desire! He is the originator of every good thing, and the only one who will truly satisfy our souls.

There are many delights in this life that offer temporary gratification, but if we choose to pursue them instead of seeking the Lord, we will end up dissatisfied and confused. The Lord has given us many good things, but they are not to infringe on his place in our lives. An example of this is our spouse. Marriage is an incredible gift from God. It is a symbol of his love for us, and we are expected to treat it with respect and care. It is a high priority that requires love and attention, but it is not our source of strength or fulfilment. God alone grants wisdom, and from him comes the understanding we need to advance in all other areas of our lives.

As you and your spouse together seek the Lord
for wisdom in your marriage this week,
what do you want to better understand?

Knitted Together

Every day they continued to meet together in the temple courts. They broke bread in their homes and ate together with glad and sincere hearts.

ACTS 2:46 NIV

Nothing cements a marriage better than spending time with God together. It's hard to go to bed angry when you kneel or hold hands and pray before bedtime. When we pray with and for each other, it provides a shield of protection around our marriages and our homes. When we spend time talking about wisdom we've gleaned from God's Word, and how it has touched our hearts, we feed our souls. When we attend God's house together, he knits our lives together with a strength beyond all worldly ties.

If you are newlywed, decide now how you will establish habits of faith. If you've been married for a number of years and haven't done it before, it's never too late to start. Your heart and your home will benefit, and you will be glad you did it.

How can you and your spouse build habits of faith?
If you have faith habits already set,
how do they affect your relationship?

Drink Deeply

With joy you will drink deeply
from the fountain of salvation!
ISAIAH 12:3 NLT

Water serves many purposes: it refreshes, cleanses, heals, and causes growth. A deep drink of water when you have been thirsty rejuvenates your entire being. In a similar but much more profound and eternal way, Christ's salvation has refreshed our weary spirits by offering hope. It has cleansed us from all our sins, it heals us from our wounds by giving us forgiveness and the ability to forgive others, and it allows for us to grow in our relationship with our God and Father.

Salvation brings greater joy than anything found within this world! There is no sensation like being washed by the fountain of salvation because its cleansing power is lasting. We are no longer guilty because we have been made pure. We are no longer hopeless or thirsty because when we drink of the water Jesus' offers, its effects are eternal.

Do you feel refreshed or weary these days?
Do you need to spend time hearing from the Lord?

Rejoicing in Suffering

Rejoice inasmuch as you participate in the sufferings of Christ,
so that you may be overjoyed when his glory is revealed.

1 PETER 4:13 NIV

No one likes hard times. They can be rough on a marriage. Financial difficulties impact every aspect of our lives. Health crises wear on us physically and emotionally when we can't help our partners. Sometimes, circumstances beyond our control create chaos in our marriages.

Suffering is hard on all of us, but joining together in those moments makes all the difference. We can make a conscious choice not to let bitterness ruin us. We can say, "God, I can't fix this. I need your help!" We turn our suffering over to him. Walking together, united with God and each other, provides the strength that's needed. Let us use moments of suffering—and God's provision through those times—to share the glory of what God does for us and through us.

*What difficult circumstances
have you gone through as a couple?
How did you react to the problem,
and how did it strengthen you?*

Pleasing Presence

How happy your people must be! How happy your officials,
who continually stand before you and hear your wisdom!

2 CHRONICLES 9:7 NIV

When the Queen of Sheba saw all the wisdom, riches, and greatness God had given to Solomon, she was astounded! Every one of the king's friends and servants alike were happy and satisfied under his rule. His kingdom was both impressive and inviting. His reign was based in compassion and justice. Imagine, then, how wonderful and powerful the Lord of Hosts is, who gave Solomon all that he possessed; both his external wealth and his internal wisdom.

How blessed we are to serve under the rule of the Lord God of the heavens! It is he who gives us everything we need; who offers us comfort, encouragement, purpose, strength, and direction. When we consider who the Lord is and what he has done, we realize true joy and untouchable contentment. He is the source of all wisdom—that of King Solomon's and our own. There is no reason to be dismayed when our hope is in God and when we are submitted to his wisdom.

In what ways are you and your spouse serving the Lord?

Acceptable Words

Let the words of my mouth
and the meditation of my heart
be acceptable to you,
O LORD, my rock and my redeemer.
PSALM 19:14 ESV

Sometimes it seems that the only safe place is home. Outside the warm circle of marriage we can be bombarded by verbal abuse, disrespect, put-downs, and blasphemy. Speak joy and life into your spouse, don't tear them down when you talk to them. Purpose to build them up with your words. It has been proven that respect, courtesy, and loving encouragement from one's husband or wife will have a marked change for the better in the relationship.

God wants your marriage to be strengthened. The words we speak have consequences. Do we purpose to build our loved one up, or do we shame them with rudeness and contempt? An interesting thing happens when we praise our spouse whether they deserve it or not: our hearts change for the better!

Do we speak with love and compassion to each other?
Do we let irritations show with put downs and derision?
Can we agree to speak purposefully to each other with love?

Cultivate Thankfulness

Be thankful in all circumstances,
for this is God's will for you who belong to Christ Jesus.

1 Thessalonians 5:18 nlt

We always have more than enough reasons to be thankful for what our heavenly Father has done for us. Even our trials are supposed to bring us joy because of what they can produce in our lives. Whatever circumstances come our way, we hold fast to the promises of God and remember that nothing can separate us from his love. The Lord's grace is sufficient to carry us through, and if we trust him with the hardships we are confronted with, he can even use those for our good and his glory.

No matter how bleak things may seem, we can conclude that we still are loved, upheld, and vindicated, and everything will work to our benefit and blessing if we can simply trust God with the outcome. Maintain an eternal outlook, trust the Lord to lead you, and remember to always rejoice and give thanks. This is God's will for us.

*How can you and your spouse cultivate a thankful mindset
when circumstances appear to be bad?*

Directing Hearts

May the Lord direct your hearts to the love of God
and to the steadfastness of Christ.

2 Thessalonians 3:5 esv

When Paul prayed that God would direct the hearts of the Thessalonians, he chose the Greek word *kateuthynai* to describe his intent. The word implies removing all obstacles or anything which would hold someone back. As we obediently allow the Lord to direct our hearts rather than be swayed by the pressures of this world, our lives will display the difference. Our stress levels will decrease, our marriages will be blessed, and we will have a deeper relationship with our heavenly Father. Learning to walk in the steadfast love of Christ will teach us how to also be steadfast in other areas of our life.

Marriages cannot continue on the basis of early infatuation; a healthy and intimate union requires perseverance, intentionality, and sacrifice. We are given the opportunity to display steadfast love to our spouses the same way Christ Jesus demonstrated it for us. Allow your hearts to be guided by him, and cling to his steadfast love.

Are there obstacles in your life hindering you from walking in close relationship with God or enjoying a thriving marriage?

Olive Branch

How good and pleasant it is
when God's people live together in unity!
PSALM 133:1 NIV

*O*ne single thought begins this psalm. David was concerned with the unity of a group of men who were close enough to be called brothers. Even though ties can run deeply in a group of people, division is always possible. This reduces the strength of a group, like an ant colony of individuals. Nevertheless, David was more concerned with the benefits of unity rather than the evils of disunity. He points to the pleasant bonds that exist in those who can live together with friendship.

It is sad that so few people truly know what unity feels like even within the church. This can probably be traced to the carelessness of actions that precludes division. The efforts needed to maintain unity are monumental with the reward being equal if not greater. Today, take time to ask God to give you eyes to see where unity is at risk, wisdom to mend it, and strength to encourage it.

What actions can you take to fight for unity in your marriage,
in your community, and in your country?

Times of Separation

I long to see you again, for I remember your tears as we parted.
And I will be filled with joy when we are together again.

2 TIMOTHY 1:4 NLT

Although Paul was like a mentor to Timothy, the two of them had a very special bond. Paul referred to Timothy as a brother, a son, and as beloved and faithful. He recognized that Timothy was distraught at Paul's imprisonment and even encouraged him to come visit. Deep friendships, such as the one shared between these two ministry partners, can bring an incredible sense of joy, encouragement, and love. The Creator intended us to be together not alone.

When we are separated from someone we care about, it can hurt. In marriage, we are blessed to be able to share our life, our home, and our ministry. That kind of bond is a gift that should be recognized for the remarkable blessing it is. With regard to close friends who are distanced from us, we should still encourage them and remind them of how much they mean to the Lord and to us. Paul wrote letters while in prison. Whatever our location or means of communication, it is important to stay connected to those who fill us with the joy of the Lord.

Who are you separated from right now that inspires you
to draw closer to God? How can you encourage them?

Glad for Today

This is the day that the LORD has made;
let us rejoice and be glad in it.

PSALM 118:24 ESV

We celebrate birthdays and anniversaries with special plans involving favorite foods, activities, and the like. To mark the day sometimes gifts or cards are exchanged. What about celebrating *today* as if it were a gift? Well, it is!

When we marry, we assume that we will have many, many years together, but this is not always the case. Some of us may be called home sooner than expected. Learn to celebrate together each day. Rejoice in your oneness. Surprise one another occasionally with a card or special meal. Make memories together. Enjoy the journey that is marriage. Be glad for today!

Are you aware of each day as it passes?
Do you take your spouse for granted?
Can you surprise one another
with special plans once in a while?

Thankful for You

> How can we thank God enough for you in return for all the joy we have
> in the presence of our God because of you?
>
> 1 THESSALONIANS 3:9 NIV

Do you use the words *please* and *thank you* when talking to each other? Don't assume your husband or wife knows that you are grateful for the things they do for you—tell them! Make it a habit to use these simple and polite words in your conversations with each other. We teach these magic words to children at an early age, but somehow when talking to the most important person in the world to us, we drop them.

Gratitude and politeness expressed to each other goes a long way. It doesn't matter if your spouse takes out the garbage all the time, they will still appreciate a simple thank you. As you get up from the table, be sure to say *thank you* for the meal. It might have been hot dogs, but your partner took the time to make it for you. Sharing gratitude shows respect for your spouse's time and efforts.

> *Can you endeavor to show respect to each other*
> *by saying please and thank you?*
> *Will you make it a habit?*
> *Can you do this without keeping score?*

Faithfulness

As for me, I shall sing of your strength;
Yes, I shall joyfully sing of your lovingkindness in the morning,
for you have been my stronghold and a refuge in the day of my distress.

PSALM 59:16 NASB

The strength of our God is most obvious in the middle of our salvation, for it seems impossible to forget him when we hear a song of forgiveness for the first time. Sadly, time dulls every memory. Just as a steadfast watchman keeps his eyes on the things to come, we must remain vigilant in remembering what has come to pass. The psalmist is crying out, "You have been my stronghold and a refuge in the day of my distress." Those days must not be forgotten but cherished in their proper place.

The days of our distress are special to us, never to be recreated. God has given us special memories of deliverance. If we have never run for cover under the refuge that is our Savior, this is the day for us to create our first memory of deliverance.

What encourages you in the morning
and prepares you for the day?

Blessing of Hospitality

Whenever we have the opportunity,
we should do good to everyone—
especially to those in the family of faith.

GALATIANS 6:10 NLT

*H*ow believable is our message of good news if our actions and attitudes are not good? If we have truly encountered the grace and love of God, our lifestyles will show it. It will culminate in us an attitude of gratitude and compassion. Whenever we are given the opportunity to do good for someone else, we would strive to take it because of the good that was done for us.

Everything good we have is from our Father; out of appreciation we extend our blessings to others. This should be especially true within the family of faith because family is supposed to take care of each other. Consider the outside world looking in: they can see how we treat each other. Why would anyone want to be part of a dysfunctional family with no unity or loyalty? Our first responsibility is to members of our own body, then to the onlooking outsiders who need love and grace as well.

Why does it seem harder to do good and show love
to Christians at times than to the lost?

Showing Mercy

Blessed be the God and Father of our Lord Jesus Christ! According to his great mercy, he has caused us to be born again to a living hope through the resurrection of Jesus Christ from the dead, to an inheritance that is imperishable, undefiled, and unfading, kept in heaven for you.

1 PETER 1:3-4 ESV

God fully equips us for the tasks he has called us to do, and Peter believed it was important that the exiled Christians to whom he was writing understood this. Since none of us were born with the capacity to love sacrificially and live righteously, we can attribute it to God bestowing these characteristics on us. We did not earn godly aptitude but received all that we require by knowing him personally and answering his call.

It is by God's power alone that we have the ability to lead a godly life; however, we still must decide to use the gifts he has given us. We have been brought from death into life and have been given an eternal inheritance with Christ. Our response in the life we have been entrusted with should be to offer our obedience, loyalty, and love to the one who saved us and gave us such an incredible hope!

How do you and your spouse encourage each other regarding your eternal inheritance?

December

Love is supreme and must flow
through each of these virtues.
Love becomes the mark of true maturity.

COLOSSIANS 3:14 TPT

The Perusal

The LORD has looked down from heaven upon the sons of men
to see if there are any who understand,
who seek after God.

PSALM 14:2 NASB

The pursuit of the Lord in any relationship is the most important thing to dedicate ourselves to. God is our solid foundation to weather us through storms and keep us sheltered throughout any trials we face. If we find ourselves in times of trouble within marriage, one of the first things we should check is the condition of our personal pursuit of God.

We should think of our marriage as an equilateral triangle with us and our spouses on the bottom corners and God on the top; the closer we draw to him, the closer we will become to each other. As married couples, we represent the relationship God has with his church. If our connection with him is weak, our representation of him will also be weak. By drawing near to him, our marriages will flourish.

Could you and your significant other seek God more diligently both individually and together?

Hard Knocks

I know what it is to be in need, and I know what it is to have plenty.
I have learned the secret of being content in any and every situation,
whether well fed or hungry, whether living in plenty or in want.
I can do all this through him who gives me strength.

PHILIPPIANS 4:12-13 NIV

Our time on this earth is like a blink of our Father's eye, and throughout our lives we will witness both poverty and plenty. The Lord provides as he sees fit and always has a plan unfolding in the background, despite how it may feel at times. During times of difficulty, we must praise the Lord for how we are being strengthened to serve him more effectively. In times of rest and plenty, we shall praise him for his blessings in our lives and use them for his glory.

Both need and plenty belong to God and he will give and take away according to his wisdom, while also providing us with the strength necessary to overcome adversity. While enduring a struggle with family, it is easy to shift to many sinful mindsets such as blaming, hopelessness, or apathy. Additionally, during seasons of plenty, it is frighteningly easy to forget the Lord who pulled us out of struggle, thus squandering the blessings he has provided. We must stay attentive to one another in the good times and the bad. If we seek the Lord for our strength, we shall never grow weak.

How has God used struggles in your life to strengthen you?
How have you gotten the most
out of the blessings he has given you?

Seek the Lord

Sow righteousness for yourselves, reap the fruit of unfailing love,
and break up your unplowed ground; for it is time to seek the Lord,
until he comes and showers his righteousness on you.

HOSEA 10:12 NIV

The good we sow will directly contribute to the love we reap. The bad we sow will also return to us. God calls us to sow righteousness just as he called Israel to. In a marriage relationship, we must be intentional about sowing good seeds, otherwise we will reap bad fruit. We must make conscientious efforts to help our loved ones in ways they would appreciate and profess our love through actions.

We can and should speak life into our marriages, but without action and effort supporting our speech, all our declarations will fall flat. Marriage is like growing a fruit tree. If nurtured and taken care of, it will yield enough for us and others to be blessed and to carry us through the droughts. If we ignore the tree and fail to provide the love and care it needs, when we arrive at times of struggle, we will not find fruit to sustain us. If we nurture our relationships by being willing to put the work into giving what is required, then we will reap the blessings of it also.

What does sowing righteousness into your marriage look like?
What are some examples of fruit it might produce?

Two Masters

"No one can serve two masters.
Either you will hate the one and love the other,
or you will be devoted to the one and despise the other."

LUKE 16:13 NIV

God should be the master of our entire lives including our relationships. Wealth, success, personal interests, and even our loved ones must fall in line after him. A healthy, godly relationship will have only one thing commanding its course, and that is the Lord who has promised to lead us in the way of everlasting life.

It is surprisingly easy to assume we are following the Lord's direction, place our attention on autopilot, and then one day look at our lives and realize that something else has been our driving force. When a man and woman come together in matrimony, they are promising to serve each other as they would serve the Lord. The goal of serving each other is to sacrifice our own selfish desires for the needs of our spouses and serve the Lord together while we assist one another in staying true to that course. Our relationships to our partners should be full of love and caring servitude, never one of master over servant.

*Is God the one guiding you through life,
or have you let something else take the reins?*

Daily Savoring

Every time I think of you,
I give thanks to my God.
PHILIPPIANS 1:3 NLT

Having someone you love more than life itself is beautiful and illustrative. Our love for our spouses points directly toward the love our Father has for us. Our loved ones are gifts from God to help us both understand him and represent him better. When our minds and our hearts are right, we cannot help but thank God for his incredible blessing of the person we love most. If we see them serving our Father, we rejoice on their behalf. When we witness their sorrow, we long to comfort them just as our Father comforts us.

In this passage, Paul is rejoicing in the faith of the church of Philippi and giving thanks to the Lord who is shaping them to be his people. In the same way, we ought to apply this principle to our own lives and rejoice when the ones we care about so deeply are similarly being used and shaped by God. We rejoice in their growth and in the glory their lives bring to our Savior.

Have you made an effort to thank God for your spouse?

Fullness of Joy

You make known to me the path of life;
in your presence there is fullness of joy;
at your right hand are pleasures forevermore.

PSALM 16:11 ESV

If our goal is to obtain fullness of joy and pleasures forevermore, then we will rapidly realize that such a goal is only achieved through following the path of life illuminated by God. A common mistake made in relationships is a shift in goals from seeking that closeness with God to seeking that closeness with the person who has captivated our attention. People cannot offer true fulfillment no matter how invested and loving they are.

The only relationship which can bring total satisfaction and endless love is with God, and the greatest of human relationships are the ones that are fully committed to and blessed by him. When two people seek the Lord together, the result will be that they become closer through their shared objective. God wants all his people to seek him, and two people encouraging each other are stronger together. Obedience to God results in a healthy relationship, life, joy, and eternal pleasure.

*Are you and your partner walking the path of life toward God
or searching for fulfillment in each other?*

Authentic Models

> "Do not look on his appearance or on the height of his stature,
> because I have rejected him. For the LORD sees not as man sees:
> man looks on the outward appearance,
> but the LORD looks on the heart."
>
> 1 SAMUEL 16:7 ESV

This verse is both fearsome and comforting. How delightful that we do not have to measure up to the world's standards to be selected of God for his purposes. And yet, how sobering to know that our true selves are completely laid bare to the King of the universe.

This is the relationship that he has called us to—to know him even as we are known. The marriage covenant is the closest earthly representation of that heavenly reality. This is the authenticity that we are called to model in our marriages. In no other interaction can we know and be known by another human being so intimately.

Are you completely transparent with your spouse,
or do you find yourself trying to cover up?
When you open up to each other,
are you gentle in your responses?
Talk about ways you can practice
becoming more authentic with each other.

Carrying Burdens

Carry each other's burdens,
and in this way you will fulfill the law of Christ.

GALATIANS 6:2 NIV

What is the law of Christ? What are we fulfilling? This verse has a fairly straightforward meaning which can be interpreted simply and accurately as "carry each other's burdens," but on a deeper level, how does that affect God? Firstly, the term "law of Christ" is used only once in Galatians, once in 1 Corinthians, and both times by Paul. This term is not defined in text, but we can interpret its meaning if we look at Christ himself. Jesus said that the most important law is to love the Lord, and the second most important is to love our neighbors (Mark 12:28-31). He seems to be pointing at the condition of the believers' hearts in both commandments.

If we serve out of love, then we are following the will of Christ. His desire is that we serve one another and carry each other's burdens out of love, which is how he treated us and how we fulfill his law. Love is the root of every commandment the Lord gives us. In a relationship, serving each other out of love is a true reflection of Christ.

How can you help carry your companion's burdens better?

Abandoning Self

"Respect the LORD and serve him fully and sincerely.
Throw away the gods that your ancestors worshiped
on the other side of the Euphrates River and in Egypt.
Serve the LORD."

JOSHUA 24:14 NCV

It may not be common to have physical idols, but there are spiritual idols that many of us serve which cause terrible damage to both our romantic relationships and our relationship with God. The Israelites were in Egypt for an extremely long time; long enough to adopt the gods of their captors. When God rescued them from Egypt and from their slave masters, he also commanded them to leave the Egyptian gods they had adopted behind. His intention was to free them spiritually as well.

Whether we find ourselves addicted and captive to worldly things like media, drugs, alcohol, money, success, or even unhealthy relationships, they all detain us from firstly and fervently following the Lord. We cannot follow two masters, so we must leave our former idols in the past and walk into the light. Doing so will help us be better partners for our spouses and more faithful servants for God.

What idols do you think you might be serving?

Personal Jesus

We proclaim to you what we ourselves have actually seen and heard
so that you may have fellowship with us.
And our fellowship is with the Father
and with his Son, Jesus Christ.

1 JOHN 1:3 NLT

Our lives preach most powerfully what we have encountered personally. John was arguably the closest earthly companion of Jesus during his three and a half years of ministry. He was among the first chosen of the twelve. With Peter and James, he was part of Jesus' intimate circle of three, and he was Jesus' confidant.

John doesn't teach others about Jesus Christ like some kind of history lesson. He introduces God the Father and the Son, whom he knows personally. This is the companionship John invites us all to encounter: the real, living God and his real, loving family.

Is your close companionship
with your spouse evident to others?
How so?
In what ways does your married life encourage others
to a personal relationship with Jesus?

Little and Great

"Whoever can be trusted with very little can also be trusted with much,
and whoever is dishonest with very little will also be dishonest with much."
LUKE 16:10 NIV

God allows us to experience trials and tribulations for many reasons. One of these reasons is that trials give us a chance to prove how much we really trust him. When we experience a difficult time, it is an opportunity to show people that we are not shaken by things of this world. When God sees his children putting their trust in him that way, he is honored, and he will entrust them with much greater tasks.

Trust is not bought or easily obtained; it is proven by constant faithfulness, humility, and sincerity. Marriage is one of the greatest ways to demonstrate our love for the Lord because we are constantly being presented with a choice to be selfless or selfish. Every day is a new chance to show we can be trusted with very little. Can you imagine the things God has planned for you, if only you prove to be a faithful servant?

How can you practice being trustworthy in your marriage?

Differences

There is neither Jew nor Greek,
there is neither slave nor free,
there is no male and female,
for you are all one in Christ Jesus.

GALATIANS 3:28 ESV

Although the Creator God designed us with a variety of features and faces, when it comes to the issue of faith and forgiveness, no one is outside of his grace. All are of equal importance and where their maker is concerned; men and women, poor and rich, all ethnicities, all backgrounds. Paul confronted the misguided idea that Christ came for the Jews only.

Everyone was made in the image of our Father. He holds the only position of power and prominence within his eternal kingdom, and we are all beloved children under him. Any reliance we have in our own supremacy and any discrimination we feel toward someone else is in opposition to the Word of God. Jesus came for the freedom and forgiveness of all, and our job is to show love and compassion to everyone.

*How can you make a point not to classify people
by their heritage, gender, or role in society?*

Unswerving Faith

Let us hold unswervingly to the hope we profess,
for he who promised is faithful.

HEBREWS 10:23 NIV

The Jewish Christians were under great persecution at the time this letter was written. They were being urged to return to Judaism and to forsake the teachings of Jesus, but they knew that their newfound freedom was only available to those who followed the Messiah. They could not knowingly put themselves back under the law and abandon the grace God had given them. He is always faithful to what he has promised, so these early Christians held fast to their hope in Christ even though it meant persecution for approximately seven million of them and gruesome deaths for about two million.

Our enemies today may not carry swords, but they are still set on destroying us and turning us away from Jesus. The death of our spirits is far worse than the destruction of our physical bodies, so with the same unswerving faith of the early Christians, we must take hold of ourselves and keep our eyes fixed on Jesus.

*Is there anything that tends to distract you from God
or causes you to engage in unwholesome behavior?*

Guard Your Heart

Above all else, guard your heart,
for everything you do flows from it.
PROVERBS 4:23 NIV

Temptation is a real and serious threat, and passive admittance of its existence is not enough to avoid its snares. Furthermore, attempting to strongarm our way through temptation will also eventually lead to our overthrow and destruction. It is only by guarding our hearts and avoiding temptation that we stand any chance to maintain holiness, and the only way to guard our hearts properly is by equipping ourselves with the truth found in the Gospel.

God fashioned our hearts and he is the only one who can protect them from the enemy's attacks. This world and all its alluring ruses threaten to undo the work of Christ in our lives, but when we immerse ourselves in the Scriptures and actively walk with God, any attempts to deceive us will be thwarted by the truth we have embedded in our hearts. When we fail and our hearts wander, God is gracious to draw us back to him and cleanse us. Seek him together and ask for his grace today.

How are you actively guarding your heart against temptation?

Always Hope

"For I know the plans I have for you," declares the LORD,
"plans to prosper you and not to harm you,
plans to give you hope and a future."

JEREMIAH 29:11 NIV

There are times in our lives when we cannot see the hand of God at work. We cannot hear his voice. We cannot discern his purposes. We can neither comprehend the greater story God is crafting, nor can we grasp our role in it. We feel abandoned and forgotten, at the mercy of chance and catastrophe.

Such was the case for Israel when addressed by Jeremiah. God had carried them away into exile as a result of their sin, but even in discipline, God had mercy. He did not abandon his people. His plans were intact. Though they could not see it, his purpose was still at work. From Jeremiah God declared hope for Israel.

*What circumstances have clouded your vision
of God's purposes in your marriage or family?
What does this passage speak to your heart
about God's greater purposes in troubling times?*

Prayer of Blessing

He took them in His arms and began blessing them,
laying His hands on them.

MARK 10:16 NASB

*J*esus made it very clear that all were welcome to come to him;
Jews, Gentiles, sinners, sick, and even children. He was not playing
the part of an esteemed celebrity, but a caring healer whose arms were
open. When the disciples tried to stop children from bothering Jesus,
he instead called them to him. The word *blessing* comes from the
Greek word *eulogeo*, which means either to celebrate or consecrate.

Whether we are parents ourselves or we have other children in our
lives, we can easily become preoccupied with labeling things childish
nonsense, yet Jesus tells us to be more like children. Instead of
negating their whimsical innocence, we should celebrate it and learn
from it. Jesus celebrated the young ones just the way they were. It is
vital to our spiritual growth that we put aside our pride, learn from
the children God has put in our lives, and go before God in a similar,
unassuming, fully dependent way. Children are not a burden but a
blessing that should be embraced.

*What children in your life have you
and your spouse been blessed by?
What have you learned from them?*

Important Things

The important thing is faith—
the kind of faith that works through love.

GALATIANS 5:6 NCV

*E*ver since the world began, God has proven his faithfulness to us. His goodness has never wavered, and his character is unchanging. We can confidently place our faith in him because he has always been and always will be faithful and true. In the moments we waver in our convictions to him, he still accepts and uses what little faith we have to offer.

With faith as small as a seed, he can move mountains. With the most meager offering of obedience, he can conquer nations. There are ample examples in the Bible of weak, broken people who he used to bring about his purposes. Being usable has nothing to do with our strength and everything to do with our surrender. Even though we cannot see what is coming in the future, we know we can trust our good God.

*How can you and your spouse
encourage each other in your levels of faith?*

Unlimited Forgiveness

"He arose and came to his father.
But when he was still a great way off,
his father saw him and had compassion,
and ran and fell on his neck and kissed him."

LUKE 15:20 NKJV

As much as we don't want to do it, all of us mess up from time to time. When that happens, we usually hurt the one we love, sometimes causing extreme damage to our relationship in the process. When you're the one who has been hurt, that can be hard. You know that God says to forgive, but how are you supposed to do that? The story of the prodigal son gives us some good guidelines. The son had it great at home and his father loved him. But he broke his father's heart when he left, and he suffered horrible consequences as a result of his rebellion. He hit bottom.

But you know what? When the prodigal came to his senses and returned home, his father didn't meet him with, "You hurt me! How could you do that?" He ran to him, grabbing him in his arms, and hugging him with tenderness. What if we loved each other like that? What if we forgave like that?

Do you have a hard time forgiving your spouse?
How can you learn to forgive like God does?

Gentle Rain

Let my teaching fall on you like rain;
let my speech settle like dew.
Let my words fall like rain on tender grass,
like gentle showers on young plants.

DEUTERONOMY 32:2 NLT

Have you ever lived in an area that experienced drought? The dirt is so dry it cracks. The grass is brown and the flowers curl up as if hiding from the heat and sun. It is difficult to plant anything because the soil is so hard. Rain is much-anticipated, but if it comes down in fast torrents, it runs off instead of soaking into the dirt where it is needed. The best scenario always arrives when a gentle rain comes that soaks into the ground slowly.

That's how God wants his words to fall into our souls and marriages. Like the gentle rain that leaves behind tender soil and plants, his words can refresh our hearts, providing wisdom, warnings when necessary, inspiration, and encouragement. Let's not have hard hearts when God wants to speak with us; let's be like the tender grass and young plants that soak up every drop.

Is your heart tender toward God?
Do you and your spouse desire the refreshing rain
of God's presence in your home?

Fixed Thoughts

Fix your thoughts on what is true, and honorable, and right,
and pure, and lovely, and admirable. Think about things
that are excellent and worthy of praise.

PHILIPPIANS 4:8 NLT

Temptation is a real enemy of our marriages and it can have a devastating effect on our homes. Whether it's a glance at someone who isn't our spouse, hours on Internet sites where our eyes shouldn't be, or temptations with gambling, alcohol, or some other substance, those moments leave us vulnerable and can cause severe damage to our relationships.

That's where we need to be proactive as couples, where we need to set up areas of accountability. Let's determine that we will "fix our thoughts on what is true, and honorable, and right, and pure, and lovely, and admirable" as it says in this verse. If our attention is captured by those things, we won't have time or the inclination to stray into areas that could harm our precious relationship with each other.

Have you struggled with temptation?
How can you help each other with that?

Important Instructions

All Scripture is given by inspiration of God, and is profitable for doctrine,
for reproof, for correction, for instruction in righteousness.

2 TIMOTHY 3:16 NKJV

It is easy to occasionally slip into a habit of reading the Bible for
the sake of the action itself and without expecting to be moved
by the experience. We start to view the Scriptures as just another
book rather than the living Word which feeds our souls and leads
us through life's most treacherous patches. The truth is that when
our hearts are open to receive the wisdom found in the Bible, God
intends to show up and change us from the inside out. Even with our
small faith as a starting point, he can transform our minds and our
hearts to receive his truth with renewed vigor.

God speaks to us through his ancient texts, but we hinder that
communication if we are simply reading and not listening. When
we are unwittingly closed to gathering new insights, God is still
faithful to break through our immaturity and shape us into the kind
of people who learn to go before him expectantly. When we learn
to turn to the Scriptures for every matter, and we recognize the
treasure this tool is, we find ourselves filled with thankfulness and
an unquenchable desire to grow closer to God. May we never take
his Word for granted.

Have you prioritized daily time to read the Bible?
If not, what is hindering you and how can you overcome it?

Hidden Word

Your word I have hidden in my heart,
that I might not sin against you.
PSALM 119:11 NKJV

*L*iving a godly life hinges on knowing the Word of God. How can we obey and follow God if we do not know what he has said? Debatable theology and disunifying views are rampant within Christendom, and they cause great confusion and division among its members. As the Biblical lines blur throughout our culture, it becomes clearer and clearer how imperative it is that we hide God's Word in our hearts. The Bible is God's will and plan, recorded so that we would understand how God expects us to live. We will experience an unmatched joy and fulfillment when we do what we are intended to do, but we can only learn what that is through prayer and reading the Scriptures.

Those who know God and are familiar with his words decrease their chances of sinning in error or of becoming confused by false teaching. The risks diminish greatly because they are wise to the Word and cannot be easily fooled. It is important to read the Scriptures and take them to heart so we remember them when making moral decisions.

What Scriptures can you and your spouse memorize together?

Contrary Living

I will sacrifice to You
With the voice of thanksgiving.
That which I have vowed I will pay.
Salvation is from the LORD.

JONAH 2:9 NASB

There will be, and possibly have been, times in our life when we have to choose God over a normal existence. Offering thanks to the Lord, declaring that salvation is through him alone, and speaking the Word of truth is not typical. This passage is one of a man who had abandoned God's path because it seemed absurd to him. Now he returns to his God with the words, "I will sacrifice to you with the voice of thanksgiving."

We may find ourselves far from God in certain seasons of our lives. At other times, our sin nature will rise up from within. In both these situations we have to decide: do we make the atypical choice and act like Jesus, or do we live as the world around us lives? At the crossroads of God's way and the way of the world, our hearts must know that salvation is from the Lord, and all other ways lead us astray.

Once you make a wrong decision, how can you turn around
and get back on track without continuing to let that decision
lead you down a dark road?

As a Baby

To us a child is born,
To us a son is given;
and the government shall be upon his shoulder,
and his name shall be called
Wonderful Counselor, Mighty God,
Everlasting Father, Prince of Peace.

ISAIAH 9:6 ESV

*O*ur Lord and Savior was the embodiment of the eternal message sent to earth from heaven. He did not arrive with a sword proclaiming justice and striking down his enemies but came as a baby to teach the weak how to love and win his enemies over with grace. The self-righteous cried out for the blood of heathens without understanding what the consequences of that would be.

The brokenhearted who Christ came to heal soaked in his words and were moved to repentance by his presence. He came into this world in the most approachable, attainable way possible. Jesus came as a leader but also a friend because his desire was to be with his people. He leads fairly and lovingly, and by his example he counsels us in the way we should go. He fills us with power to do what is right and he brings peace to our anxious hearts.

What did Jesus have to teach us by coming to earth as a baby?

The Messiah

"Today in the town of David a Savior has been born to you; he is the Messiah, the Lord."

LUKE 2:11 NIV

The Lord Almighty did not owe us salvation. There was no requirement for him to take on humanity, subject himself to the miseries of life and death, and become the perfect atonement for our sins. Not only was he willing to undergo all of this, but he did so with great joy because he knew that the outcome would be our freedom. His love for us is beyond measure!

The manner in which he was born, lived, and died each demonstrated the greatest humility a King could ever possess, and a deeper love than any human has ever known. He came to overthrow death, erase the stains of sin, and set free the captives, but he also made friends, healed the sick, and communed with his people. There is no way to fathom or explain a love like this; we can only choose to gratefully accept it and pronounce him Lord and Messiah.

Why did Jesus come as a baby?
Why did he come first to Bethlehem?

Perfect Faithfulness

LORD, you are my God;
I will exalt you and praise your name,
for in perfect faithfulness you have done wonderful things,
things planned long ago.
ISAIAH 25:1 NIV

*U*pon first encounter, this verse seems uplifting and straight-forward. Although it is that, there are several other layers to it as well. It holds a clear testimony of who God is and what he has done for us. The important aspects of praise and adoration are professed. It clearly acknowledges that God is our Creator and the source of everything which exists. We, like Isaiah, acknowledge his reign over us and all that concerns us, and we accept his infinite love and care for us.

Praise from a thankful heart is what God desires, so when we go to him this is exactly the kind of attitude we should bring. As the sheep of his pasture, let us worship and bow down before him. Let us bring our praise, our hurts, and our questions to him for he desires to be all things for us. God has done many wonderful miracles; things he had planned long before even the creation of the world. We are indeed loved.

What is something wonderful that God has done for you
which you would like to thank him for today?

The Sword

> The word of God is alive and active. Sharper than any double-edged sword,
> it penetrates even to dividing soul and spirit, joints and marrow;
> it judges the thoughts and attitudes of the heart.
>
> HEBREWS 4:12 NIV

*M*ost of us want to be the best spouses we can be. But for that to happen, God has to smooth away the imperfections. He has to cut out the things in our hearts that shouldn't be there. He has to get through all the muck until he reaches our hearts and souls. He doesn't just judge our actions, he judges our thoughts and attitudes as well.

That's where God's Word comes in. The Bible isn't an old book to be left on a shelf or on the coffee table collecting dust. The words in it are alive, and if we'll read them with the right heart attitudes, those verses can seep into our souls, replacing the messed-up things there with pure and clean thoughts and a heart that wants to please and honor God. Reading his Word together as a couple will provide a strong bond that won't be easily broken, and as we see each other striving to please God, it will deepen the love that is already there.

Do you read God's Word with the right attitude?
How will that affect your marriage?

Consider the Creator

When I consider Your heavens, the work of Your fingers,
the moon and the stars, which you have ordained,
what is man that You are mindful of him,
and the son of man that You visit him?

PSALM 8:3-4 NKJV

We experience such exhilaration while exploring the wonders of nature, yet often disregard the Creator from whose imagination every natural wonder originated. We fail to give him credit and forsake any exploratory notions of realizing him. Like any of us, God wants to be known and desires a relationship with us. He is neither drab nor boring, but creative and powerful. The mountains and the oceans were his idea, as were the clouds and the stars.

Mesmerized humans will even misdirect worship toward the heavens, falling short of the one who rules them from his heavenly throne. Far more brilliant, majestic, and exciting than any of the wonders we have witnessed in the world is he who fashioned them all. Even more incredible is the realization that he created it to share with us, and that he has chosen us to be the recipients of earth and the inheritors of heaven!

When you consider your marriage and how wonderful it is, do you consider the one who created it and brought you together?

Rule Followers

Joyful are people of integrity, who follow the instructions of the LORD.
Joyful are those who obey his laws and search for him with all their hearts.

PSALM 119:1-2 NLT

Some people are rule followers. For them, a rule is a rule and there is no question about whether or not to follow it. Other people have a harder time following the rules. But no matter if it is hard or easy for you, rules are there for us to have parameters by which to play games, drive cars, live life, and so much more. When others know you are a rule-follower, they know you can be trusted and that you will do the right thing.

Trustworthiness is of supreme importance in marriage. When you promise to love, honor, and cherish, you are also promising to trust your mate, even if the exact word is not in your vows. You are becoming one in every way with another individual, and you are committing to being trustworthy. Both of you will find tremendous peace and joy in knowing the other can be trusted.

Are there areas where you find it difficult to trust your mate?
Resolve those issues today.

Foundation

> "From the beginning I told you what would happen in the end.
> A long time ago I told you things that have not yet happened.
> When I plan something, it happens. What I want to do, I will do."
>
> ISAIAH 46:10 NCV

From the time of Adam and Eve, God planned marriage to be a union. You can trust your marriage has twined the two of you into one. It may have been love at first sight, or perhaps you slowly got to know each other and friendship became romance. It doesn't matter; God had plans for you. He formed the foundation of your love. Build upon that foundation.

If you are newlyweds, you may wonder if you will have children. If you are new parents, you may wonder what college your child will go to. Older parents may wonder about empty nests. Whatever stage you are in, it is normal to question what the future holds. Enjoy the present. God will take care of you no matter what the future holds.

Are you missing out on the present in your marriage?
Are you so busy worrying about the future
you are failing to pay attention to your spouse?
How can you make each day important?

Led by God

I praise the LORD because he advises me.
Even at night, I feel his leading.
I keep the LORD before me always.
Because he is close by my side,
I will not be hurt.

PSALM 16:7-8 NCV

It is difficult to live without direction, without purpose, and without instruction. Like a ship on the ocean without any control, we would be hopelessly lost without God's Word to guide us. If we did not have the counsel of the Scriptures to save us from the devil's schemes and the world's wickedness, we would veer off in the wrong direction and be dashed upon the rocks.

This psalm offers reassurance that if we keep steady with the Lord we will not be overcome when the waves begin to crash. It is certain that trouble will come into our lives, but we can also be certain that God will be with us in those moments, and we will have nothing to fear if we keep him before us. Holding fast to him is the safest place we can be, especially in a world that is uncertain and confused. Without God, there is much to be feared. With God, we have eternal security, unbreakable confidence, and unending love.

As you and your spouse prepare for this coming year,
have you asked God to go before you?
Do you trust him to lead you and take care of you?